Declutter and Organize Home Handbook

—————— ❧❦❧❦ ——————

Over 100 Tips to Get Your Life Back on Track to Enjoy Beautiful and Inspiring Spaces

Chloe S

and utter responsibility of the recipient reader. Under no circumstances will any legal responsibility or blame be held against the publisher for any reparation, damages, or monetary loss due to the information herein, either directly or indirectly.

Respective authors own all copyrights not held by the publisher.

The information herein is offered for informational purposes solely and is universal as so. The presentation of the information is without a contract or any type of guarantee assurance.

The trademarks that are used are without any consent, and the publication of the trademark is without permission or backing by the trademark owner. All trademarks and brands within this book are for clarifying purposes only and are the owned by the owners themselves, not affiliated with this document.

Contents

Manuscript 1

Minimalism

————— ✌︎❀✌︎❀ —————

The Practical Minimalist Strategies to Simplify Your Home and Life

Chloe S

Introduction

I want to thank you and congratulate you for purchasing the book, *"Minimalism: The Practical Minimalist Strategies to Simplify Your Home and Life"*.

This book contains proven steps and strategies on how to filter and shed the excess stuff and live your life with purpose. The philosophy of minimalism can be applied to any part of your life: what you own, what you do for work, what you put on your calendar, and how you relate to and connect with other people.

Minimalism is not about living in a tiny home and never owning more than 100 things (though you can certainly do that). To live as a minimalist does not mean you have to give up modern conveniences. There is one guiding principle for deciding what stays and what goes: figure out what brings value and purpose to your life and let go of the rest.

Applying this principle is not a one-size-fits-all approach. Each of us—individuals, couples, and families—will use this policy for our particular season and situation. We will have different answers to the question of what brings value and purpose. You are reading this book because of your interest in minimalism. You also probably suspect that our culture's intense pursuit of having more and doing more doesn't lead to lasting happiness. Like me, you want to set about discovering how less means more in your life.

Minimalism helps you reassess your priorities so that you can identify and strip away the excess that doesn't line up with what you want. Although the journey often starts with removing physical clutter, it also leads you to let go of the clutter from your heart and soul. It brings awareness to the void in your life that you're trying to fill with things that will not fill it, at least not for very long.

Thanks again for purchasing this book, I hope you enjoy it!

Chapter 1:
An overview of minimalism

History of Minimalism

The minimalist movement was one that began in 1960's America in the art world in response to an art culture that had become cluttered and overblown. Minimalist artists of the time considered that the overuse of symbolism and metaphors in art had become excessive and reacted by creating a new form of art which focused on the materials of art, rather than the message.

For example, instead of painting canvases overloaded with hidden meanings and symbols, the minimalist might create a sculpture from a discarded piece of pottery or paint a portrait of a lone red square. The point was to make a return from the endless searching for meaning through motifs in art and instead embrace the simplicity of the essence of art; its materials and raw form.

The point was to create works with no concealed references to politics, history, current events or hot topics, but to create jobs which were beautiful in their simplicity simply.

Music followed suit. A 1964 composition by American composer Terry Riley named merely In C is widely considered the first arrangement of a minimalist music piece. As in the art world, music compositions had become overloaded with unnecessary instruments and layers, creating music that was ultimately unpleasant to listen to and an assault on the senses. The minimalist movement in music was a return to more straightforward harmonies with fewer instruments that allowed the listener to appreciate every note.

Fashion, too, embraced the movement. Minimalist fashion follows the same rules as in art and music; namely rejecting any design which is over-complicated or covered in any logos or images which refer to any subject and draw attention away from the everyday and straightforward form of the garment itself. Many people think of minimalist fashion to mean wearing nothing but all black or all white and having no accessories, but real minimalist style goes even further than this, with designs that may be very complex to tailor being considered minimalist because ultimately, when worn, they appear to have streamlined, simplistic forms.

Alternatively, minimalist fashion can seem bizarre as it may go so far as to even reject the form of the body itself and therefore garments can be deliberately designed to draw attention away from the figure of the wearer.

Of course, after the minimalist movement was adopted in the cultural spheres of art, music, and fashion, it was embraced by interior designers all over the world. Minimalism in interior design evolved a little later than minimalism for music, art, and fashion, but has become a favorite style across the globe.

The fundamental principle of minimalist interior design is 'less is more' and has been influenced by styles from homes all over the world, especially from interior design styles in Japan. Minimalist homes are devoid of clutter and use color sparingly and in a block rather than using patterned wallpapers or murals, for example.

While interior design embraced minimalism in the twentieth-century, the architecture of buildings was becoming minimalist in design from as early as the 1920's. Minimalist structures often use geometric shapes such as domes and triangles in their design and materials such as glass and steel to prevent buildings from being over-stimulating to the eye.

In the modern world, minimalism can be seen in the designs of technological devices, such as streamlined laptops and TVs with no visible buttons or controls. Over the last century, minimalism has been adopted in some form in every visual culture.

However, the movement has grown from there, and there are people today who consider minimalism not to be merely an aesthetic ideology, but a way of life. The philosophy of a minimalist lifestyle is to live without all the non-essentials in life, such as excessive material belongings and flashy cars and homes.

Now, the minimalist lifestyle may not have originated directly from the visual cultures we have spoken about, but the ideals are primarily the same, and often the minimalist visual cultures come hand in hand with a minimalist lifestyle as a whole. Some people would say that their minimalist's belief stem, preferably, from a Zen or Buddhist approach to life, whereby attachment to material possessions is obstacles to true happiness.

For others, an excess of possessions or the demand of household bills and chores became detrimental to the lifestyle they truly desired; lives that are full of travel and easy mobility. For these people, material possessions act as an anchor to tie them down and prevent them from freely moving through life. For others still, a minimalist life is sister to green living, whereby the real intent is to reduce our impact on the earth by becoming less reliant on consumerist goods.

What is Minimalism?

To find out if the minimalist lifestyle is for you, ask yourself these critical questions:

- Would I be able to live without so many material possessions?

- Would my life improve if I owned less material things?

- How would reducing the clutter in my physical and mental space affect me and those around me?

How you answer these questions will show you the path towards creating a minimalist lifestyle. In a shopping-obsessed, materialistic society, is it possible to live well, be happy and resist the need to buy things you don't need?

I'd say yes! I'm going to show you exactly how. How you can enjoy life, reach inner peace and lead a fulfilled happy life – with fewer material belongings, less mind-clutter and less harmful energy.

This book is divided into several parts that represent different areas of life. Under every section, you'll find chapters or sub-categories with real-life advice related to the region in question.

To help you, even more, we compiled a month's worth of small, yet meaningful steps for living a minimalist life. They are all simple, easy and effortless things you can do to try out if this lifestyle suits you; also, they're things that many minimalist people do every day in all areas of their lives.

Minimalism is a mindful practice. It is why we coined the phrase, 'The Mindful Minimalist.' It's about being grateful for what you own, knowing what you need (which is different from what you want) and using it to clear your mind, improve your relationships, and thrive on simple things rather than drown in possessions. Ultimately, it's about being happy with who you are and what you have now.

I invite you to read this book apply the advice you'll find here as you see best.

Why Choose Minimalism?

Now that we explained the primary purpose of minimalism, you're probably curious about why you should choose the minimalist lifestyle. You're probably inclined to ask more questions:

- What good will it do for my loved ones and me?

- Will I be happier if I decide to become a minimalist?

- Isn't it a bit radical to suddenly change my life and get out of my comfort zone?

- Will I be able to get used to spending/having less?

Let us try and answer them for you.

Minimalism isn't living in a sterile, dull, monotone environment. In fact, it is the opposite. The way you create your minimalist life depends entirely on you and your priorities. The underlying philosophy behind minimalism is to bring you more financial, emotional, material, and physical clarity and freedom. When you make space for the truly relevant things and people in your life, all other areas will start to follow as well.

People who are not familiar with the minimalist lifestyle can sometimes view it as radical or fringe. But once you realize and become aware that you don't need excess material things to make you fulfilled and happy, it's not even close to radical. It's simplicity. It's the ability to live a simple life and find meaning and joy in the things that you prioritize.

Some people embrace change, and their transition to a minimalist lifestyle is easy, and they get used to it quickly. There are also people whose adjustment to change takes time and effort. So, the answer to this question is something you'd have to estimate according to your personality. If this lifestyle suits you and you feel lighter and better because of it, you're sure to get used to it and enjoy it.

Here are some key reasons to embrace minimalism:

- You will no longer be owned by your possessions. Instead, you'll learn how to select which ones are necessary and essential and which are just mere clutter;

- You'll gain a sense of freedom and liberation from the pressures of "modern" life. You'll understand that success comes from within – from your feeling of fulfillment and not from having an enormous home, several cars, comfortable clothes, and jewelry or social status.

- You'll spend less money. And that's a good thing. Spending less on things you don't need means saving pay for things you do need. And that's called financial freedom.

- You'll feel more productive. Decluttering your mind, life and home, as well as your working space, can contribute significantly to productivity. All the energy that comes with an over-stuffed place will go away, and new, fresh one will take its place. It'll bring you positivity, fresh ideas and a feeling of openness and will-power.

• You'll learn not to get attached emotionally to material objects. Instead, use that energy to connect with the people you love. That's way better for your well-being than any item you'd buy.

• The reduction is the keyword when adopting a minimalist lifestyle. Expect to reduce significantly the number of items that you and your family own. These will be items that are not essential for surviving and living – mostly; they're items that you bought as an impulse purchase, things you keep "just in case" you ever need them, things you buy in bulk so that you're never out of something and basically, anything extra. This creates room for air, energy and essential elements.

• You'll have more time to devote to your hobbies, family, and health. This is one of the best benefits of the minimalist lifestyle – your time will be occupied by the things and people you love instead of struggling to buy more things that you don't need. Objects can't love you back – people can.

- The minimalist lifestyle inevitably brings peace. However, some people fear the future because they're afraid that if they don't have something, they won't be happy, they'll suffer, or they'll end up miserable. Minimalism is not poverty. It's just living a simple life. Money in the bank is always better than having no money and lots of possessions.

- Minimalism doesn't restrict having things. It just teaches you to shop more substantially. Spending less (or not at all) on unworthy items leaves you more money for things that'll bring value and positive change into your life.

When all benefits combine, the result is a happier, more fulfilled and more meaningful life. To sum up, the overall philosophy of Minimalism is in approaching your way of life and how you think about the physical things you own. Do the material attributes you hold in your life empower you to live out your dreams or are they restricting your time and energy? Is the maintenance, organization, and storage of your items giving your more time or less? Let the Minimalist philosophy inspire you in this journey of being more and having less.

The transformation of your current life to a minimalistic lifestyle can seem slightly daunting. This is because you're about to make a significant change in habits, consumption, finances, and your overall life. Though you know this difference is for the better, you're still scared of how it will all turn out.

Fear of the future and how your life will unfold is normal. You think you'll have less, when in fact, you'll have enough. If you've never experienced the minimalist lifestyle firsthand, this is probably your primary concern.

To build a minimalist life, first, you need to think like a minimalist. To do that, you're going to need to simplify your mindset, your ambitions, emotions, and desires. Declutter your mind to make space for new, positive thoughts and empowering mindsets. Then, you can go on and plan your minimalist home, room decor, food, work, *etc.*

Your mind creates your life. It establishes the "needs" and the "wants," and it leads you to achievement. I'm sure that during the reading of this book, you either thought or will think that you could never give up on some things. Because you're so emotionally attached to them and you don't want to lose the beautiful memory that those objects remind you of.

There's a very simple revelation behind this philosophy: memories are formed in your mind and stay in your heart forever. You decide to associate them with objects, and if the purpose is not present, you fear that the memory will fade away. However, fears, like limits, are often just an illusion. The reality is your mind is capable of keeping the memory alive for as long as you choose to. This is the exact reason why people tend to keep so much stuff – it's their treasure full of experiences they hold dear.

If you are still not convinced, we have a minimalist hack for you. If you have an item that has no practical use but holds a treasured memory, try this: Take a picture of the thing, and you can look at it anytime you want without it taking up physical space.

So, if you think you could never give up on TV, your car, your too-many-bedroom home, your closet full of clothes and shoes, your favorite junk food and more – think again. Your mind can adjust to and adopt anything – in this case, the minimalist lifestyle that will bring you a lot more positive changes than your current life does.

What follows are some simple steps, tips, and tricks to build a minimalist mindset:

• Recognize and select your needs. Often, people don't distinguish between what they need and what they want. This is true of material things. For example, we don't need a new appliance – we just want it because we think it'll make our life easier. We don't necessarily need 2-3 cars – we just want them for the same reason. The list goes on How much cabinet, pantry, and counter space all of your instruments occupy? Many machines are not used frequently enough to make life easier. Though a device may initially expedite a cooking task, count the amount of time it takes to clean and reassemble the apparatus after the function.

• Eliminate the "just-in-case" mentality. Much of the clutter in our homes comes from hoarding items that we don't need immediately; rather, we think we might need them in some hypothetical future. We keep those items "just in case" fearing that we won't survive without them. Examples of 'just in case' items to eliminate are all those extra wicker baskets, various craft items. Another way to define 'just in case' items would be non-essential items (Examples: wicker baskets, various crafts, impractical shoes, or stacks of pens you keep). Contrast that with essential items such as fire extinguisher or first aid kits.

• Take your time. Becoming a minimalist is a massive change, and it doesn't happen overnight. Gradually, you'll start to realize how this lifestyle works and adjusting your expectations should be by the process.

For some people, it might happen in a couple of weeks; for some – a month or two and others, it might take longer. Have faith, keep your goals in mind, and everything will fall into place.

• Practice. The beginning may be hard, especially if you haven't tried minimalistic living before. The key to a successful transition is to practice. Start small. Get rid of things you haven't used in years (Especially three years or more); clean the garage; your pantry *etc*. With practice, you'll learn to select objects and classify them as essential or non-essential.

• Make a list of pros and cons. Be honest, objective, and view the question as if it wasn't your own. This can significantly assist in the process.

• Being a new Mindful minimalist will take time and patience. Through this process, you will begin to value people more, objects less, and live life like never before. You will feel freer, as you only let go of all these non-essential items burdening you.

Why simple living is important

As humans, there are essential things we need to survive. We need clothes to keep us warm. We need food to nourish our body. We build homes for shelter.

And then there are things that he wasn't in life, for recreation and consumption.

Today, however, most of us want things that didn't exist before. These things could bring joy and satisfaction, or unnecessary obsessiveness and addiction. The Internet has brought us unlimited information about the world around us. If you wanted immediate access to movies, you have Netflix. Instead of collecting music albums, you can download hundreds via iTunes. If you wanted to look smart, a digital bookshelf of literary classics could work its magic for you.

We can talk to people despite long distances. We can take our work anywhere. You can work on multiple things at once across several screens due to the onslaught of so many apps that could do anything. Life and work become more efficient, fast, and practical.

But progress has its pros and cons. We are bombarded by advertisements that reshape our desire for material possessions. We want bigger houses, faster cars, more advanced technology, fashionable clothes, expensive cuisine, and more.

Consumption is necessary, but in excess, it is not. Many of us work harder for things we may later realize we don't necessarily want. Owning too many things hampers not only our movements but also essential priorities. These priorities a back seat until we understand later that we have lost so much time in pursuing stuff we don't need.

And because of technological advances, we are expected to do more work since everything is almost automated. This leads to the habit of multitasking. It also doesn't help that the current addiction to screens drives most of us to have less sleeping hours, more stress, and unhealthy habits.

Do you feel like you are one of those people mentioned above? Are you working hard but feel like you are not accomplishing much? Do you realize that many of your possessions are stealing too much of your money, time, energy, and focus?

This can all be changed, but you must change from thinking about decluttering your physical environment and your mind. The first step to achieving this is to have more space to move about and to help clear your head. You need to be in an environment where you are not always stressed out because you have too many things to do, or because you don't have enough time to work on your goals and to be with the people you love.

I believe you will agree with me when I say that most of us desire to live comfortably and well-balanced lives. We all want space and enough time to reflect and decide how we want to spend each hour within a day and our future. This necessity for reflection is something that has been lacking in our modern life. We need to pull ourselves back to realize what is important to us.

And all this can be done by applying the concept of Minimalism

Chapter 2:
The Minimalist Mindset

Minimalism appeals to a desire for a simpler life—an uncluttered and unbusy life filled with more meaning, purpose, and joy. This is a healthy desire and pursuing it can lead to many benefits. Who doesn't want clarity of mind, financial freedom, contentment, a happy home, and better health, just to name a few?

The *Why* of Minimalism

It's important to know why you want to pursue minimalism. Having a firm grip on your *way* to becoming minimalist will be a steady source of fuel for your motivation to be one. This matters as much for those who are just beginning this pursuit as for those who have been after this for a while. And as you experience a minimalist life, you'll likely find new reasons to be minimalist. First, I want to tell you what I mean by *minimalism*.

What exactly is Minimalism?

Minimalism is a trade

When I think about minimalism, I don't think about what I must give up. It's not about setting a limit to the number of things I can keep. Instead, it's about what I'm trading. Giving up something is always about trading.

When we shed our excess possessions, we're making room for something better. *Everything has a cost.* When we say yes to one thing, we are saying no to another. A minimalist life is about trading a life filled with clutter, busyness, and noise for a life filled with meaning, connection, and purpose.

Minimalism is living with intention

When you apply the philosophy of minimalism to every part of your life, you practice intentionality. You ask yourself questions like: Do I need this? Will this bring me joy? Does this grow my character? When we approach our day with the intention of discovering what brings happiness and contentment, every subsequent action is filtered through this lens of conscious purpose.

Minimalism is awareness

As you apply minimalism and intentionality to your life, you start noticing how the powerful messages of our culture have influenced your past and present decisions.

You may be questioning the value of what you've filled your home with, the work you've chosen, and even the way you connect with other people. Are you spending everything you have in time, energy, and money on possessions, work, and relationships but still longing for more? Go back to less to find more of what you're after.

Minimalism is freedom

Like it or not, we humans tend to make things more complicated than they need to be. We compare our lives to those around us and start thinking we should have what they have, do what they do, and be more like them. Minimalism helps you break free from keeping up with anyone else around you. It enables you to discover what matters more for you and your family. It shifts your focus from what everyone else has, does, or is, to what satisfies you. We are free to focus on what matters when we're less distracted by all the noise and clutter around us.

The soaring cost of excess stuff

I invite you to think about your stuff for a minute. Think about the things that you own but don't use and may not even like now. Ask yourself if there are some things that you've forgotten that you own. How much time have you spent acquiring and taking care of things? As Henry David Thoreau said, "The price of anything is the amount of life you exchange for it."

We spend a lot of time on our personal belongings. We store them, clean them, find them, repair them, wonder if they're worth fixing, replace them, wonder what model to replace them with, consider what accessories to get with them, and search for the best deal for them. As you can see, personal belongings not only take up physical space but mental energy as well.

Let's face the reality that our deeper, heartfelt desires and goals aren't satisfied by more material goods and a jam-packed calendar. We're probably looking at diminishing returns in this crazy pursuit of *more*—spending our limited resources of time, energy, and money on homes overflowing with stuff and schedules overflowing with commitments, only to be left wanting more. Our overflowing calendars magnify the cost of our favorite material. The busier we are, the less time we have to take care of all of it.

There are tangible costs of our stuff, like money and space, but the higher prices are psychological. In today's culture, material goods have become substitutes for deep and meaningful connections. We strive to acquire possessions and busy calendars, and then ignore the things that give us lasting fulfillment and joy: personal growth, contributing to others, generosity, and healthy relationships.

The actual cost of our excess stuff and chaotic lives reaches far beyond a price tag and a full calendar. Our excessive consumption is killing us and the people we want to be. I encourage you never to underestimate the benefits of removing things you do not need.

Chapter 3:
Importance of Minimalism

The less we have on our plate, physically and mentally, the more energy and gratitude we can have for the life we want and the life we have! When people think about the benefits of minimalism, they often think only about the initial interest, such as an uncluttered home. But there are life-changing benefits to gain as you move past the initial purging. It isn't just a simple, clean home we're after. We're trading our excess stuff for things we'll look back on and wish we had more of, like time spent pursuing our passions and purpose and in relationships that bring positive transformation.

Minimalism directs your finite resources of attention, time, energy, and money toward being and doing more of what matters most. With this foundational benefit, you are better able to make the intentional choice to be and do who you're prepared to be and what you're made to do. This benefit is not just for some individuals who have the freedom to make drastic changes in their lives. All of us—including you and your family—will gain from it.

1. Less stress and anxiety

Our excess stuff is most likely affecting the stress levels of our children. The excess visual stimuli are a distraction for them as well. Less to take care of means less to stress about, and this can help us find more clarity of mind. Once the initial dopamine rush of getting something is gone, clutter becomes a constant brain drain. Using MRIs and other diagnostic tools, research has found that confusion hurts our brain's ability to concentrate and process information.

Finding more clarity of mind is possible as we clear away the distractions that come with keeping more than we need and trying to be someone we aren't made to be. Just making a start on this path can give your mind more bandwidth with which to focus on what matters most in your life.

2. Stronger relationships

Humans need to connect with other humans—we don't want to be lonely.

A minimalist home and lifestyle help us put our focus on people, instead of on the stuff they have. There are more energy and space for people and relationships to flourish.

We don't build satisfying connections around possessions—not even shared properties. Links are established around shared experiences. I'm not saying that territories have nothing to do with our relationships. But when we use a lot of our finite time and energy on properties, we're spending time connecting to our stuff and our schedules more than we are relating to other people. Minimalism is making a conscious choice to use things and love people because the opposite will not bring us the connections we long for.

3. Healthy boundaries

Minimalism helps you set healthy boundaries by giving you the clarity to see all the things you're spinning your wheels on. Resetting boundaries to align with priorities is an ongoing process in a minimalist lifestyle, but it's not an unwelcome chore. The rewards of more being and less striving encourage me to keep going on this journey. If I don't prioritize my life, someone or something else will.

4. More time

Keeping more than we need, whether its possessions or activities, brings a fog into our daily lives that make it harder to think clearly. Under the influence of clutter, we may underestimate how much time we're giving to the less critical stuff. Minimalism helps you see how you're spending your time and to think more clearly about how you would like to donate it.

We've found gap time in our family since we began practicing minimalism. This means we aren't living in the land of rushing around between one activity and another. Minimalism has helped us identify the actions, even the perfectly good businesses, which take us away from better things. We no longer feel the pull to participate in every sport and enrichment activity that could benefit our children. Remember, this is a good thing.

5. Less stress about finances

Financial minimalism has given us the freedom to share with those who benefit far more from our excess than we ever will. But we aren't just giving away money or things that we don't need as much as others do. We're giving up money and possessions that we only don't need. Not only do we not need it, but this excess is also at the very least a distraction, and at worst costs us more to keep than to give away!

6. A streamlined home

Imagine having a home filled with no more than what adds value to your life. When you de-clutter, you're more likely to know what you have in your home. Finding what you need when you need it becomes a more manageable task when you develop clutter-free habits. Less frustration means less stress. Like a lot of other people, I strive to live in a clean and uncluttered home but don't want to spend all my free time cleaning it. Having less stuff covering our floors, furniture, and kitchen counters has cut my cleaning time in half. Less time cleaning is more time to do something we enjoy more.

7. Environmentally friendly

We waste less when we buy less, and this is good for our planet. For the average American, clothing is cheap and readily available. One result of this is that the average American now generates 82 pounds of textile waste each year. Although I love a deal as much as anyone else, I no longer take pleasure in unnecessary clothing purchases at my local Target.

Minimalism has helped our family take steps toward a zero-waste lifestyle. Just because we still need a weekly garbage pickup doesn't mean we can't or shouldn't keep taking steps to reduce our waste production. When possible, we choose products that can be used for a lifetime. For example, we discarded our plastic water bottles in favor of stainless steel ones. Since we each have and use our water bottle, we keep plastic out of landfills and have fewer dishes to wash every day. Environmental minimalism helps you cultivate earth-friendly decisions, like choosing sustainable and recyclable beauty products, canceling your catalog subscriptions, choosing electronic media for books, magazines, and newspapers, switching to online banking and digital record keeping, carpooling or using mass transit, and limiting your shower time.

A minimalist home produces less waste, which is good for our planet and all of us living on it.

8. Deeper spiritual life

Many of us make a journey of faith to discover what we truly need and who we are meant to be. A spiritual journey can be interrupted by having too much and by having too little. Minimalism nurtures growth and discovery of who we are expected to be. Busyness is likely to give us a false sense of purpose and materialism is expected to provide us with a false sense of being blessed. We might not call it materialism when we post our pictures and stories with the hashtag #blessed on Facebook, Twitter, or Instagram—we probably want to express our gratitude and highlight our moments of happiness. But we can show our appreciation and contentment by giving what we don't need to someone who does need it. We can pursue and share our real purpose when we say no to commitments that don't serve it.

9. Freedom

Ultimately, minimalism gives you freedom. Freedom from consumerism, debt, and anxiety about caring for your possessions. Freedom from the weight of sentimental items. Freedom from guilt to keep things that no longer serve your purpose. Freedom from holding on to your fantasy-self and from measuring up to unrealistic expectations. Freedom to relax and think about what you want to think about. Freedom to say no to additional obligations and to make better connections with family, friends, and neighbors. This is what minimalism is genuinely about.

Chapter 4:
How to Live a Simple Minimalist Life

Most people think that they can accumulate a lot of possessions and still be able to live the dreams that they have. But the problem is that this is not true. Things only get in the manner of being able to live a life where you are free to do what you want and free to do as you please. You need to understand that if you're going to live a life of freedom, then you are going to have to take the time to look at how the things you own are holding you back. Once you come to this realization, you are going to be able to get rid of the things that are doing just that. Then you are going to be able to spend more time on the things that matter to you.

The first thing that you need to do is look at everything that you own carefully and examine what is required and what is not. You need to see which items are used on a regular basis and which are rarely if ever used. Once you have done this, you are to throw out, donate, or sell all of the items that you do not use and keep all the things that you do use on a regular basis. This is the initial and most crucial step toward you achieving the life you want.

Next up is to make sure that you do not bring any more clutter into your home. This means that you stay away from places where you usually buy things for the sake of it, like a shopping mall. If you need to buy an item and you see that you are going to use it on a regular basis then and only then buy it. However, you will come to see that most of the things that you think were necessities were just impulse buys that would have resulted in more crap entering your home. That's all there is to lead a more simple minimalist life.

Get Focused

Before you ever embark on a new journey, it is important to get focused and clear on what you are doing. You want to know precisely why you are taking on a new adventure or path, and what this lifestyle will mean for you. Getting focused gives you the opportunity to completely understand what your motives and intentions are and why you should stay committed when things get difficult, which they always do at one point or another.

With minimalism, you should understand that the lifestyle is more than just living a life free of physical clutter. It is also about living a life free of mental, emotional, and non-physical clutter. You need to learn to stay focused on what you want and stop dwelling on things that do not serve you and have no purpose in your life. You can do that by getting focused and staying clear on what your goals are.

Initially, getting focused might be extremely simple. There are usually two reasons why someone wants to become a minimalist: either they cannot stand looking around at clutter anymore, or they cannot hold all of the restrictions on their time. Because both of these involve stress and discomfort, people are driven to make a change in their life. However, it can be easy to stop making changes once you reach a place of comfort. Or, you may not want to begin because you realize that any difference will be less comfortable than what you are already doing. After all, we tend to stay in lifestyles that are most comfortable to us.

It is crucial that you learn that staying focused and determined takes effort on a constant basis. The focus is a balancing act that you must work towards regularly. The more you work towards it, the more success you are going to have with it. The following tips are going to help you both with getting focused and clear on your path, and with learning to re-center your focus along the way. You will be guided through a couple of journaling exercises which will give you an excellent opportunity to get clear and provide yourself with something to refer to when it gets difficult.

These activities are essential to your success, so it is a good idea actually to invest the time in completing them.

Decluttering methods

Decluttering is essential to starting a minimalist lifestyle. It might seem a shame to get rid of perfectly good items, but there are several ways to justify decluttering so that you don't feel guilty. You need have no qualms about throwing away things that are worn, stained or no longer useful to anyone. Some of your quality stuff can be passed on to people you know. If a friend has often remarked that he loves a particular figurine, something that's not all that important to you, give it to him so he can enjoy it.

You can also donate items. Goodwill, Salvation Army, and other non-profits receive donations and accept almost anything. A Habitat for Humanity ReStore will be glad for your discarded household fixtures.

You can always hold a garage sale and make a little bit of money while getting rid of things you do not need; you can get to know the neighbors in the process. You can always give away or throw away anything left over. You will be surprised what people will take when it is free. Some non-profits will even pick up your unsold items at their thrift stores.

There are multiple methods available to help you declutter. I suggest you try out several and pick what works best for you. Decluttering does take time. Don't assume to get it all done in one day but do set goals to guide you through the process. I suggest you use a calendar to mark down each stage of your decluttering and assign them specific target completion dates.

It's easiest to tackle the process one room at a time. Be aware that cleaning out a closet will usually take most of a day or even two days; it's a big job! Decluttering the kitchen is also a one- to a two-day job.

Some experts say you should do a little decluttering at a time, giving one item away per day or filling one trash bag in a week. Others say it is all or none. They think you should go through every closet and drawer with clothing in it all at one time, so you don't forget what you have.

Remember, you make the rules. If you want to take it slow, take it slow. Just keep in mind that one item a day means it may take your life to complete the decluttering process! However, if you are enthusiastic about becoming a minimalist, get it all done in a week or two and start enjoying your clutter-free lifestyle?

The following are some popular methods of deciding what to discard, with techniques for staying organized during the process:

The 12-12-12 Method

Twelve is a nice round number. It doesn't take long to gather up 36 items and decide what to do with them. To work the 12-12-12 method, you collect things in your house, finding 12 things to put away, 12 things to give away and 12 things to throw away. You can do this once, twice, or three times a week. It's up to you.

The Four Boxes or Baskets Method

Acquire four large boxes that are nearly the same size or go out and purchase four of the same kind of laundry basket. One will be for trash you will throw out, one is for things to give away, one is for things you want to store, and the fourth is for things you want to keep. Take a room and start filling up the boxes or baskets. Once you fill them, get rid of the stuff in the trash box, box up the things you want to give away, then pack and stash what needs to be stored. Take everything out of the fourth plate and ask yourself, "Do I need this? Does it bring me joy?" If the response is yes, then put it in its proper place; otherwise, put it in one of the other boxes.

The Mapping and Rating Method

In this method, you make a map of all the rooms in your house. Mark where the doors and windows are located and draw in the closets. Draw where the furniture sets. Rate each place as to how cluttered it is, marking one for uncluttered, two for somewhat cluttered, three for very cluttered, and four for the last cluttered space. Start with the most cluttered room first and take that map with you.

Mark with an "X" the most cluttered area and start cleaning out there. You can use your 12-12-12 technique or the four-box method in conjunction with this plan.

Acquire Financial Freedom.

I know that many people argue that money is not everything or money is the root of all the evil... etc... But well, this is not true. According to several studies and research work on wealthy people from all around the world, it is now proven that if you are financially free, then you are happier than those people in your age/income group who are not economically free.

Of course, Money cannot buy happiness. But still, up to a certain level of joy, Financial Security is essential. Most of the people are scared of being broke or even bankrupt after their retirement or even before that because of the substantial debt.

In China, most of the people worry about their debt while sleeping at night rather than heart disease and diabetes. This is the scenario of people from everywhere around the world. But people that are Financially Free are not worried about these kinds of financial uncertainties, and that's why they are happier than others in the same age/income group.

Financially free doesn't mean that you should be a millionaire or multi-millionaire. It says that your monthly Passive Income from your various Investments such as Stocks, Bonds, Gold, Real Estate & Businesses or even salary is much more than your monthly expenses. Thus, also suppose if you stop working today, you can live for the rest of your life on the Income you generate from your Investments.

To obtain financial freedom, you must master your inner thoughts and spoken words. Your innermost thoughts are the start of everything that you create. What you focus on expands. Fear-based feelings will manifest themselves into reality if you allow them to grow in your mind. You should concentrate on the things that you want so that it expands and demonstrates in your life. Your words are also crucial as negative words such as "I can't afford it" or "I will never be rich" will send out the wrong message. The universe only responds to thoughts and words of abundance. Other things like creating a spending plan, setting financial goals, learning to invest or even simplifying your life all stem from this simple idea of mastering your inner thoughts.

A word about financial worries

Many people worry about money, how to pay the bills each month. Consumer credit agencies and credit card companies have made it all too easy to run up staggering amounts of debt, offering consumers large credit lines with enticingly low monthly payments.

Many don't realize that the exorbitant interest rates that can come with such credit can put them in a deep hole financially, causing daily worry and stress.

One solution: You can cut up your credit cards, close your accounts, and make a three to five-year plan to get out of debt by living on a budget, within your means, and paying off each credit card bill, starting with the highest interest one first.

Sure, it will take time. But if you're focused on the goal of being debt-free, you can do it, and, often, just knowing you've stopped running up bills and embarked on a plan to get out of debt and build up a savings account instead can make you sleep better at night.

If you feel overwhelmed and you are past due to everything, and bill collectors are calling every night, there's still hope. Contact the folks at Consumer Credit Counseling. There's a branch in almost every medium to large city, and they will help create a recovery plan for you.

Then, they'll contact each credit agency and negotiate a payoff plan for you. If you're in a small town, you can sometimes pay an attorney to settle the payouts for you, anything to stop the interest rates from continuing to bury you under a mountain of debt.

Just remember that no matter what your current situation is, you still have a choice in how you will respond to it. And bear in mind that your present condition need not extend forever. Getting depressed is not the answer. Taking proactive steps to solvency is, and the moment you do, you will feel a massive weight lifted off your shoulders.

That's what making a new plan is for relieving the current stress and looking forward to a modern day. Choose leniency and personal forgiveness toward your past behavior, coupled with a firm resolve not to keep making the same mistakes over and over.

Enough counsel about addressing financial wrongs. Personal finance is only one of many issues or circumstances that may be clouding your mind and keeping you from happiness.

Adopt a Unique Spiritual Outlook

I believe firmly that we all have the power within us to achieve peace. All we have to do is learn to live in the Now. This is a state I try to attain regularly, with limited and tantalizing success. You can, too, by practicing the precepts outlined below.

In this section, I will try to sum up the book's teachings, in the hope that you will find Tolle's precepts enlightening. Tolle encourages us to "observe the thinker" inside all of us. By doing so, we can willfully still the many voices going on in our minds at all times. He does not mean that because we all have an inner dialogue going on inside our heads most of the time that we are crazy or schizophrenic.

He merely means that we can learn to calm that inner dialogue and achieve inner peace, something I believe most of us wish to do at one time or another. He says that experiencing the joy of Being does not come at the expense of clear thought or an awareness of the things around us. Preferably, the state of Being is one of hyper-awareness of our surroundings, a sense of being fully present at the moment. "And yet, this is not a selfish state, but a selfless state. It takes you beyond what you previously thought of as 'your self.' That presence is mostly you and, at the same time, inconceivably more significant than you."

Tolle says that 80-90 percent of most people's thinking is not only repetitive and useless, but because of its dysfunctional and harmful nature, much of it is also detrimental. "Observe your thoughts, and you will find this to be true. It causes a serious leakage of vital energy."

He says that the more significant part of human pain is unnecessary. "It is self- created as long as the unobserved mind runs your life." Tolle stipulates that if you no longer want to create pain for yourself and others, then you must realize that the present moment is all you have. He adds that we should always say "yes" to the Now.

This bears out what we said earlier about living not just one day at a time, but one hour, or one moment at a time, avoiding the possible cares and dangers of the future, and not dwelling on painful happenings or relationships in the past.

Minimalism by lowering your expectations

I once had a friend who told me something wise, "Lower your stress by lowering your expectations."

At the time, I had evolved into something of a perfectionist. I had moved into middle management and expected excellence from myself and those who worked for me. I may have been, looking back on it, something of a pain in the neck to those around me.

I also had developed a fair amount of stress, trying to control many factors that were beyond my control. I didn't want to "lower my expectations." To me, that was tantamount to accepting poor performance in myself and others. Eventually, I got older, and I began to understand the wisdom underlying this concept.

The case for lowering your expectations

In a new study, researchers found that it didn't matter so much whether things were going well. It questioned whether they were going better than expected.

Not that you should walk around gloomy all the time. Having expectations at all, say for lunch with a friend, can lift your spirits as soon as you've made plans.

Take action! This week, reset an expectation. What is a more realistic and enjoyable goal? Then, refocus on the journey rather than on the destination. What mountains can you climb that you will genuinely enjoy climbing (figuratively speaking), whether or not you ever make it to the top? How can you focus on the present moment, whatever you are doing right now, rather than setting big goals and expectations for the future?

In personal relationships, having realistic expectations will allow you to accept the flaws in others. We need to take responsibility for our lives before we can expect others to do the same.

One of the most significant challenges we face in life is learning to accept people for who they indeed are. Once you realize that your expectations cannot change people, the better off you will be.

Someone else I once heard of had a great way of summing this philosophy up: "Give without expectation, accept without reservation, and love without hesitation." It's all about perspective

Lower your expectations if you want to be fulfilled. Raise them if you're going to make things more efficient.

You can start an exercise regimen to feel better about yourself and achieve contentment. You can also contact well about yourself by taking even a few small steps to improve your self-image. This will give you renewed confidence and boost your self-esteem.

But you must be realistic about the goals you set or the exercise will be one that ends in futility. You must understand your goals clearly and map out the steps necessary to reach them.

Finally, one counselor I read about says her clients are stressed, and then they're stressed about being stressed. Well, meaning people tell them to "get more sleep or exercise" or "start a meditation regimen."

Again, does this sound familiar?

This counselor even says that having some degree of stress is standard, as long as your coping skills can deal with it. That's funny. People who can cope successfully with stress have no need of self-help books on ways to reduce stress. I have often marveled at such people, who must have a hereditary or prominent gene that allows them to slough off the weight that would kill us mere mortals.

Look within yourself

Amanda Christian, writing in the blog tinybuddha.com, says many of us want things because of the way we think they will make us feel. You may wish to a skinnier body because you think it will make you feel happy and loved. You may want a successful career because you think you will feel fulfilled. You want a relationship because you think it will relieve your loneliness.

These things can distract us from looking within ourselves for answers. When they fail to do what we want, we feel disappointed and angry. To release this cycle of disappointment, we need to release the belief that they will save us.

Relax more, judge yourself less

Christian says she learned that the loving voice within, also known as our inner guide, has a bigger plan for us than we have for ourselves. "As it turns out, right now you are exactly where you need to be," she says. The only thing you need to do, Christian adds, to follow the path of your inner guidance is listen to it by releasing your judgments about what you think is happening. You don't have to have everything figured out right now. "Get quiet and listen for guidance about what to do at this moment. Any advice coming from love will be something you can do now. The thought of doing it will make you feel lighter and excited."

Change your thoughts

The first thing I do when I feel any disturbance to my peace of mind is say to myself, 'I am determined to see this person/situation differently.' This is how you step into your power. Everything happens to you, not to you.

You'll be amazed at the shifts in perception that occur when you become willing to release fear and see love instead.

Minimizing Your Home

When you are busy, you do not have a lot of time to devote to getting your home organized. It is then easy for it to get messy, and for the mess to get out of control. It can be challenging to understand where to begin, so to help get you started, here are five quick tips to declutter your home -

1. Do not put off until tomorrow what you can do today.

Procrastination does not make it go away. In fact, it only gets worse and causes you more stress in the long run. Once you had bit the bullet and got on to it, you will feel so much better. Nothing beats looking at a room that is as neat as a pin and looking very attractive. The best part of it is that you have the satisfaction of a job well done.

2. Decide when you will start and how long you will work for before you start. Then stick with it.

Be realistic and make your goal achievable. As you complete the first session successfully this gives you the impetus to get started on your next meeting. Begin by planning what you want to achieve and how, and you can save yourself a lot of time. By setting a time limit for each session, you will still have energy left for the other things you need or want to do.

3. Donate items that you no longer want or need.

If you have some belongings that are still in good order, consider giving them to charity and free up the space they took just lying around, collecting dust. The good thing here is that you do not need to spend any more time maintaining and taking care of them, which gives you more time for other things. It is easy to hoard stuff, in case it comes in handy one day, but let's face it if it is not being used it can't be needed. The other advantage is that most charities are happy to take your donations, and they can be tax deductible as well!

4. Do not spread clutter from one room to another.

It can be straightforward to pick up an armful of clothes and take them down to the bedroom, dump them on a chair and, leave them there! Stuffing all your shoes into your closet or putting a pile of paperwork on a shelf to 'clear' the table is only moving one mess from one place to another. This can make things worse, not better or tidier! You are still not creating any free space and, you will even need to sort those piles out at some point in time.

5. Decide to handle each item once.

Allow yourself enough time to work through one problem area at a time. When looking at the things you are sorting decide where it is going and then put it in its place. The lesser ways you handle an item, the faster you get through decluttering your house. Sometimes it is not possible to touch something only once, but minimize as much as possible how many times you pick up any one thing. As you find a place for each item, it then is more comfortable to keep things tidy, because each element can be put back in its place after use. This has the added advantage of then being able to find those items when needed, saving lots of looking time.

So there you have it - 5 quick tips to declutter your home. They can help you get started quickly and make good progress, but to keep your place decluttered, work on developing it into a habit.

Chapter 5:
Minimalism and happiness

1. Lessen Your Dependencies

We all have our crutches to lean on, unfortunately for lots of us we become dependent on one or more of them. By far the most apparent crutch in our society is alcohol. It is deemed acceptable to become intoxicated or drunk primarily by the younger crowd, and the most common reasoning for the behavior is because 'it feels better to be drunk than not.' That is just an example, and the crutch could be anything, drugs, painkillers, and coffee to name a couple, usually some substance. If you are experiencing hard times and you find yourself turning towards something such as alcohol then refrain from doing so, you will only become dependent on it to get you through hard times rather then relying on yourself. Dependencies create weakness, the more you lessen your dependencies, the more you can strengthen your mind which will allow you take on larger and larger obstacles calmly and without breaking down or losing control of yourself. Which in turn leads to greater control, confidence and of course happiness.

2. Listen to Some Post-Rock

This is related to both relaxing and writing a journal as it achieves similar things. The key is to listen to soothing yet complex music, classical, acoustic, ballads anything goes here but Post-Rock is perfect. Some bands to check out for this purpose are Mogwai, Explosions in the Sky; This Will Destroy You and Russian Circles. Now why do this you ask, it's simple, most of the music people listen to is high energy or tightly focused on a subject of interest. This sort of music is naturally relaxing, and your interpretation creates the subject, it can excite your imagination, emotion and your thoughts. Similar in a way to writing a journal in that your thoughts can lead you places you didn't think they would go, similar to relaxing because, well, it's relaxing. So just throw on a track or two and sit back or lay down, just let yourself go, you may find your mind refreshed afterward. I've also heard it can help soothe people to sleep. If there is anything music can't do, let me know, it can create some happiness.

3. Meditate

This is a prevalent way to decrease stress and increase happiness. If you are not doing it already, then you should start now. Every waking moment we are bombarded with external stimulus whether we notice or not, and our brains must sort through it all at near-instant speed. What meditation does is try to minimize all the stimulus to your brain, create focus, and give your brain some 'me' time. Now you might be thinking that that is what sleep is for but not entirely. When we sleep our body re-energizes itself, and our brain churns through all the information from our day, organizing it, deciding what is essential and what is not so although we wake up fresh and may not know it our brain has been working the entire time. Meditating is easy, only lay down with your hands by your side or sit in a comfortable position then close your eyes and try to blank your mind, you can either focus on only your slow rhythmic breathing or repeat a single phrase or word over and over that is personally significant to you. Do this for about 15 minutes, and you will come out feeling refreshed and better than before, done daily meditation can work wonders for you and of course increase your happiness.

So there you have it, another three good ways to increase your level of happiness. Try not to rely on your crutches so much, listen to some nifty music like Post-Rock and meditate daily. Just remember that as with everything don't go overboard, like going cold turkey on your crutch, neglecting to listen to your usual music or building a meditation annex onto your house.

Chapter 6:
Minimizing your life for peace of mind

Just breathe - So my most significant discovery in my so-called "quest for peace" was how powerful, simple breathing could be. If you feel overwhelmed with the world, just breathe. It will release all of your stress and tensions. If you have forgotten why you wake up every morning and why you try so hard, just breathe. It will put your mind back into focus. If you feel like you can't stop worrying, just blow. It will calm you and stop the worrying entirely. Radically, breathing eases the body while also bringing your mind to the present. So next time any negative feeling(s) overcome you, just breathe.

Purge all of the clutter- Look around you right now. How much clutter is there? Confusion gives your mind the feeling of oppression, Going a little deeper. Why do we have trouble in the first place? Fundamentally, the confusion stems from our inability to let go of the past. It comes from emotional attachments to objects that have significance to us. Living in the past is unhealthy. Start off by putting a lot of them away and work from there. An open workspace with limited clutter does wonders for your creativity and peace of mind.

Find time for yourself- Artist's masterpieces are usually done in solitude, philosophers were often known to venture alone into the woods for extended periods of time, although time with loved ones is a precious gift of life. I believe time alone is almost as valuable. Alone time allows you to organize and unwind your thoughts. It will enable you to find yourself and to become at peace with the self you found.

Find time to disconnect- I love technology, but it's undeniable that it does a toll on your peace of mind. So to put it just, when you're feeling even the least bit overwhelmed, turn off the TV and read a book. You can also turn off your internet and go for a walk or as I mentioned earlier, just breathe.

While this may sound like a highly rational new way of thinking, in my opinion, it is the devolution of the old 20th-century mindset. Our collective society cries out, "Buy! Keep! Collect! What if it becomes valuable? What if you need it? What if Aunt Petunia comes over and asks what happened to the honey jar she gave you from her garage sale pile?" There is so much societal association between possessions and happiness that we cling to the things in our lives that merely drain us of our desire to do...well...anything!

Compulsion to Clutter

I have a good friend who has a shopping compulsion. This particular friend has boxes and boxes of makeup she never uses, piles and piles of clothes she has purchased but never worn, drawers stuffed full of lotions she has used once or twice, but never used up.

What is it about having things that make us feel secure, even to the point that we will refuse to get rid of a broken appliance or keep boxes of old pens and pencils that we never use? Why do magazines like Real Simple sell millions of copies annually by filling their pages with ideas on organization and tidiness, rather than tips on how to stop buying?

We keep items out of insecurity, fear, and, sometimes, genuine happiness. We buy and keep things that we think will make us happy. Whether it is just one more type of blush, medicine that expired five years ago, or another wooden snowman, each of those items, when we put it in the cabinet or on the shelf, symbolizes the happiness we are trying to achieve in our lives. But do they bring joy, all these things?

Nothing More than Feelings

The truth is one you probably already know but have heard so many times that it has lost its power to impress you. The fact that money cannot buy happiness, that things cannot make you feel secure. There are no words new enough, is no turn of phrase witty sufficient to make it a unique concept all over again.

Or is there?

Look around your home. When you do, does a feeling of accomplishment, an air of tidiness dominate? Do you feel like you have the things you want and there is nothing out of place, no item that you are keeping "just in case?" If so, feel free to skip this chapter and move right on to another one of interest.

But if you are perusing this book, probabilities are there is something about your environment that makes you feel uneasy, unable to relax, or downright suffocated. You may dream of having the ability actually to have a clean home with a minimum of effort. You have probably heard of the half-hour clean-up, but believe it is a mythical beast like a unicorn or Griffin. If that is the case, consider viewing each of your possessions on an individual basis in light of this attitude:

Does this item add peace and happiness to my life, or does it create a feeling of unease?

This may sound like a bizarre mystical kind of idea, but the truth is, everything you have does create either a positive or negative feeling inside of you when you look at it, use it, wear it, sit on it, or touch it.

This is not a statement of an enlightened mind, but merely an observation. Whether your taste runs toward the minimalist bent or the profoundly eclectic, something about each item around you sparks an emotional response. You may have to create a little more difficult about some issues than others to determine which feeling they arose, but ultimately, you like or dislike every individual piece in your home.

How relaxed you feel in your surroundings is directly related to the number of things in your environment that you like or dislike.

I want to take a moment to put my foot down hard on the brakes and add a disclaimer: That does not mean that the only way you can feel relaxed is to spend thousands of dollars to create an ideal environment.

Chapter 7:
Possession and minimalism

To achieve more freedom and more pleasure you will need to try to maintain minimalist principles, i.e., omitting needless things, identify the essential, making everything count, etc. To achieve extreme minimalism, you will learn many things about being minimalist and try to maintain the things which you should follow such as to start by realizing you already have enough, cutting back on clutter, slowly edit everything and possessions and simplifying your schedule.

Minimalism is just a fancy word for keeping your life simple and setting your priorities straight. Being minimalist is a way to achieve balance in your life. By limiting yourself in life to what is essential to my existence, you will have more time for yourself. You will have more time to exercise and cook nice dinners again. You will be able to focus on career goals that matter and not only cranking out the next widget.

The path to a minimalist life is not an easy one. To achieve extreme minimalism my home will be:

a. Less stressful

b. More appealing.

c. Easier to clean.

d. Minimal furniture.

e. Clear surfaces.

f. Quality over quantity.

The description of a minimalist office will be varied for every individual. The most last minimalist post, I imagine, would be to possess no papers or desk or computer or anything of the sort- only yourself. You would believe an utter and maybe lie on the floor.

With extreme minimalism, finances don't have to be one of the most complicated things in your life. To save money, I follow some things that I use cash not credit. I always try not to buy anything unless I need it, and only if I have the money. I think the first best step secret to happiness you can take to be content, right here, right now, is to quit purchasing useless physical things that you consider them to make you happy and the second best step you can take is to start eliminating the clutter in your life. Do this until you've pared down your possessions to the absolute necessities of your life.

Chapter 8:
30 Days to Simplify Your Life

Day 1: Declutter your online life (and stay offline for a day). Just imagine the free time to think more creatively, do productive things, or to spend it with the people you love!

Day 2: Make a list of 3-6 focused goals and priorities for the year.

Day 3: Observe and analyze your daily habits. Are they right for you? Are they productive?

Day 4: Clean the closet. Find inspiration in the Minimalist Wardrobe part of the book.

Day 5: Clean the junk drawers in the house.

Day 6: Limit or entirely give up the TV for a day. Again, minimalism is about gaining back your time wealth which is our only non-renewable resource. Recommended reading on time wealth is 'Rich Dad, Poor Dad.'

Day 7: Recycle whatever can be recycled or throw away that random item (s) that you can't remember its function. (Examples: random chargers, cords, etc.)

Day 8: Pick a corner or two in the house and remove at least one item that doesn't belong there. The more, the better, but start with 1-3.

Day 9: Gather your kids and clean the toy chest together.

Day 10: Get rid (or donate) or sell (eBay, Craigslist, etc.) 2 of the "just in case" items.

Day 11: Toss at least 15-20 items you don't like, need, use or keep "just in case." Use the 24-month rule. If you haven't used or even picked up an item in 24 months chances are they are "just in case" items.

Day 12: Start the day with meditation. Keep your TV, computer, internet, and other electronic devices turned off until lunch, even at work if you can help it.

Day 13: Clean the kitchen. Raid the pantry cabinet and toss everything you haven't used more than 2-3 months such as unhealthy, refined, sugary, fatty foods, *etc.* Refer to the Minimalist Home part of the book for tips and tricks. (We recommend the "4-Hour Body" for help in eating habits and overall health and exercise hacks.)

Day 14: Place your shoes in one place and think carefully about them. If there are pairs, you haven't worn more than once, either donate them or give them away. You can always find useful advice in the Minimalist Wardrobe section of the book for help.

Day 15: Items with sentimental value. If you're not ready to live without these items, consider making something of them. Create a DIY project for them and put them together as one.

Day 16: Wear absolutely no make-up for the day. If your profession doesn't allow this, choose one of your days off and keep a clean face. You'll instantly feel the difference and lightness on your skin.

Day 17: Today, commit to not buying anything for 24 hours straight. No exceptions to this rule.

Day 18: Clean the bathroom thoroughly. This also means going through the drawers and cabinets and getting rid of everything that you don't use, need, or doesn't belong in the bathroom.

Day 19: Create a simple morning ritual that you can stick to. (Aim for 5 minutes of meditation, exercise, reading, etc.)

Day 20: Analyze the last five purchases. See if these items were something you needed or just something that you bought on sale or because you liked them.

Day 21: Downsize on your commitments. Face the fact that they take up a lot of your valuable time and that you'd be better off without them. It's hard to say no to friends and close ones, but eventually, they'll move on, and you'll feel liberated.

Day 22: Organize a happy day. Today, you're not allowed to complain – just to be grateful. Write down the things that bring you the most happiness and be thankful for them. Forget about the things you don't have. It's one of the leading principles of a mindful minimalist (but it's also authoritative life advice) – to be happy here and now.

Day 23: We've all been multitaskers at one point. Today, try to take tasks one at a time. Hard if you're used to the rush of getting things done as soon as possible. But today, take it slow and dedicate your full attention to one thing at a time.

Day 24: Make your bedroom heaven-like. It should be the calmest and most relaxed room in the house according to Feng Shui, so take the time to make your bedroom a place where you can unwind and enjoy yourself. There shouldn't be electronic devices or a TV in the bedroom. A simple bed, nightstands, lamps, and a closet are excellent. You can have a small library if you want to read before bed but keep the décor simple. All flat surfaces should contain 2-3 pieces of décor or pictures with frames. The walls should be clean, in a soft color and if possible, with no views. Keep one alarm clock in the bedroom and get rid of the rest.

Day 25: Do the laundry without thinking about it being a dull, boring activity. The task is not to just do the laundry, but to accept its nature. Don't think of it as an arduous task. Just grab the basket, load the machine and leave. That's it.

Day 26: Go for a nice, relaxing walk. How many times have you taken intentional strides rather than walking (rushing) to the store? Very few, I know. So, today, ask your loved ones to join you for a pleasant walk around your neighborhood.

Day 27: Take a look at your finances. Is there anything in the past month that you bought but shouldn't have?

Day 28: Use your day off to relax, spend time with your family, have some fun or indulge in your hobbies. Don't work on your day off. (No e-mail peaks, answering a quick call, etc.)

Day 29: Go out and have fun. Go somewhere new, where you don't need to spend tons of money to have a good time. Go to a park, play mini-golf, or meet a friend for coffee.

Day 30: Remember and briefly journal about the past 30 days. It's not going to be perfect, but it's a pretty good start. Note: if you had any problems sticking to the plan or think there's a particular area to improve, you could always upgrade it the next time.

Chapter 9:
Tips and tricks to
minimalism

1. Write down your Reasons

The very first step to getting clear is knowing precisely what your reasons are for becoming a minimalist. You need to understand what is compelling you to make the change, and why you are so dedicated. It is essential that you are completely clear on why you are making these changes and that the reasons are important to you. When we are passionate about our purpose, we are much more likely to succeed in what we set out to accomplish.

While you are getting clear on your reasons, take out a piece of paper and write them down. Some people may benefit from merely writing this down on a page in their journal, whereas others may want to take some time with it and turn their reasons into a piece of art that they can keep in a highly visible spot each day. What you choose to do will be up to you, but the most important thing is that you have your reasons readily available.

When you embark on a new journey in life, it can be easy to have mental "relapses" which will draw you back into a previous way of thinking. You may fall back into old habits or patterns and think "well, just this once!" But it's that exact mindset that leads you towards having a cluttered environment. It is during times like this that you want to go back to your written list of reasons and feel into them. Feel the emotion you put behind them and let it rise to the surface for you. The more you can genuinely feel those emotions, the easier it will be for you to remember why you are a minimalist and stay true to your desires.

2. Reclaim Your Time

So much time is wasted when you are trapped in a lifestyle that is solely focused on acquiring the latest and greatest. You spend several hours working, often at a job you don't even like. This generates stress, grief, anger, frustration, and other unwanted emotions that you must face on a regular basis. Then, you must spend time maintaining all of the objects you have acquired. You need to organize them, reorganize them, clean them, service them, and otherwise preserve them. Then, you need to find the time to use them, which you likely rarely ever do spot, so you often end up acquiring objects that merely sit around for you to look at. If you travel or go anywhere, you likely bring more than is required just because you are too guilty to leave something behind knowing that you spent your precious money on it, which is a direct symbol for a time in your subconscious and potentially even in your conscious mind. Then, of course, you must invest time in acquiring more. So, you spend several hours in stores and malls getting frustrated over lineups, other shoppers, and anything else that may upset you. You may go into debt to acquire new things, or you may merely scrape from paycheck to paycheck because you don't want to stop purchasing new belongings. It can be a complicated trap to get stuck in.

Being a minimalist means that you get to reclaim your time. You get to stop working so hard to earn money to pay for items you don't have time to use, much less appropriately maintain. You get to stay spending hours a day working to pay off debt, cleaning, and staring at your house full of unused objects. You had the opportunity to thoroughly free yourself from all of the burdens that come along with these actions, both emotionally and physically. Ultimately, you get to reclaim your time to live a life that you want. You can do anything you want with the time that you retrieve; the choice is entirely up to you.

In the beginning, it is a great idea to take a page from your journal and write down all of the things you wish you had time for. What do you want to do that you haven't done because you don't have time? What are the things that you have been putting off because there never seems to be a spare moment for you to complete them? How are you suffering in your own life because you don't give yourself enough time to enjoy it? This list is something you should refer to on a regular basis. As you adopt the minimalist lifestyle, you will want to start checking things off of this list. If you ever feel unsure of what to do or where to go next, use this list as an opportunity to guide you. You can even build on the record as new ideas come up, regardless of how far or deep into your minimalist journey.

The most considerable part of being a minimalist is all of the free time you have. Many minimalists are even able to reduce their hours and go down to working part time instead of full time because they only don't need all of the extra money and they would rather spend time enjoying their life. Many even get to quit their job altogether and pursue a career that they are passionate about because they are no longer fearful of what will happen if they don't have a job to return to should anything go wrong. The freedom that you gain from minimalism is unparalleled, and it is something you can look forward to enjoying your minimalist journey.

3. What Do You Value?

A significant part of the minimalist journey is learning about what you value most. When you are clear on what matters most to you, then you know exactly how to spend your time and resources on creating a life that you love, which is what minimalism is all about. You should spend some time getting to know what you value and becoming clear on it.

A great way to do this is to take your journal and start journaling. Write down what matters most to you, and what you want to gain from life. What experiences make you feel productive with joy and happiness? What makes you excited to wake up and experience each new day as it comes? These are the things you want to enrich your life with. You should give yourself the opportunity to experience these as often as possible. When you are a minimalist, you have less to worry about in regards to taking care of your belongings and gaining more. Instead, you have the gift of more free time, which means that you get to spend your free time however you want.

The other reason why it is essential to know what you value is that it allows you to decide what you want to purchase and own in life. For example, if you appreciate the ability to hop in the car and go anywhere then you may want to keep your car, whereas if you don't mind taking public transit, it may be more beneficial if you get rid of your vehicle. The same goes for virtually anything else you may own.

4. Saying "No"

Learning to say "no" is essential, and it should be one of the first things you learn as a minimalist. You need to know how to say no to bringing more belongings into your house, how to say no to keep belongings in your home, and how to say no to doing things you don't want to do.

Many people believe minimalism is all about items, but it's not. It's about your time and your lifestyle as well. It is about eliminating anything that does not serve your highest good and learning to say no to anything that does not bring you joy. You want to learn how to say no and mean it, and never waiver in your answer. There is never a good enough reason to do something that does not make you feel good overall.

Saying "no" can be hard at first, especially if you are not used to doing it. The more you practice, however, the easier it will be. You should learn to say no to smaller things first: shopping, bringing jobs home, joining e-mail newsletters, and other more accessible things. As you get used to it and it becomes easier for you, you can start saying it to

5. Minimalism is a Journey

Minimalism is a journey, not a long goal. You are not going to wake up one morning with a trophy on your shelf because you 'accomplished' minimalism. Instead, minimalism is a lifestyle. You are going to be working towards your minimalist lifestyle for the rest of your life, or until you no longer desire to be a minimalist. But fear not, if you aren't already in love with it most people find that they do become passionate about minimalism and therefore it becomes easier to maintain the journey as they go on.

Any good lifestyle is a journey. As such, you can expect that your minimalism path will have ups and downs, the ins and outs, twists and turns and all sorts of unexpected events. Nothing will go as planned, and in most instances, that is the beauty of life itself. These are just some of the things that you can look forward to enjoying during your minimalist journey.

Knowing that minimalism is a journey is very important. It means that you are not going to go into it thinking that you will master it or that it will all become more comfortable overnight. While it is comprised of many skills, it is not something that you can just learn and then walk away from. The balance that is required to maintain a minimalist lifestyle takes constant maintenance to ensure that you are not depriving yourself of your basic needs, nor that you are overindulging in things that you do not need. You will always have to maintain this balance using tact, mindfulness, and practice. But, as with any pleasant journey, it is entirely worthwhile if you stay committed to the process.

Minimalism is a beautiful opportunity to learn about yourself and the things you love. You gain the ability to become the person you desire to be, and you can have any experience you want in life. The first part of mastering your mindfulness journey and your skills is to realize that you will never thoroughly learn them. Then, you need to get focused and find ways to stay focused on purpose of your journey. Once you have, you will be ready to have any experience you desire in life. The money, time, and resources will be available to you because you have gotten your priorities straight.

6. Store Things Out of Sight

Many people feel compelled to store things on the counter, or in a space where they can grab it and then toss it back down. While this might be convenient for the grabbing it part, it can also be inconvenient for the rest. After all, rolling things back down often leads to mess, and the mess is likely what lead you to minimalism, to begin with. The first thing you need to do is learn to store items properly.

Ideally, you want to store things out of sight. In drawers, cabinets, cupboards, and closets is a great place to keep items that you aren't using every single day. This means that you do not have to look at it, aside from when you want actually to use it. The key is to make sure that when you are organizing things back into these out-of-sight places, that you are still keeping them organized and under control. You do not want to have them cluttering up your out-of-sight areas, as this will merely lead to more stress. Instead, put them away in an organized and logical fashion. This keeps everything out of sight so that your physical surroundings are cleaner, and it remains everything easy to access and use.

7. Reduce Cooking Time

Many people dislike cooking for lengthy periods of time. If you love cooking and don't mind cooking on a regular basis, then this doesn't apply to you! However, if you dislike cooking and often find yourself eating "convenience" items that are costly and take up space, it might be time to learn how to cook without spending so much time doing so!

Meal prepping is a great way to get a bunch of cooking out of the way so that you don't have to worry about cooking so much on a regular basis. You can prepare meals for a few days at a time so that all you have to do is heat them up and eat them! Another great idea is ingredient prepping. This means that you pre-peel, cut, chop, slice, dice, cube, and store items in a way that makes them easy to cook with. That way when it comes time to prepare, you merely grab enough to melt with and begin the cooking process!

8. Delegate

Not everything has to be done by you. It may feel like you have to do everything alone, but the reality is that you do not. You can easily delegate tasks elsewhere so that you have more time to focus on you and what you want to and need to get done. If you have family living with you, this is

80

easy. Only create a chore-list, and everyone has their unique tasks that they are expected to get done to keep the house operating functionally on a daily, weekly, and monthly basis.

If you live alone, on the other hand, it may be a bit harder to delegate. However, there are still tasks that you can transfer out. For example, if you hate grocery shopping you can order groceries right to your door. There are many services available that offer local-delivery of fresh ingredients. In fact, you can even find services that will deliver locally-sourced organic items that are healthy and convenient. You can also delegate other tasks as well, depending on what you are looking to charge. Some people even hire maids or housekeepers with all of their spare money, to keep them from having to do any of the extra work around the house!

9. Take Breaks

Taking regular technology breaks is essential. As a society, we spend an enormous amount of time attached to devices. Our screen time racks up fast, and we often don't even realize it's happening. Between all of our unique tools, it can be easy to lose time in the online space. A great way to reclaim your time is to take regular tech breaks.

Tech breaks mean that you put away all unnecessary technology for a period. You might do daily tech breaks for a few hours per day, 24 hours break once per week, or even longer breaks. Exactly how long you choose to take tech breaks and how often is up to you, but it is recommended that you take them frequently. This gives you an opportunity to recall how to experience joy in life, without having to rely on the instant gratification of technology that often does not serve our highest good.

When it comes to taking tech breaks, you want to eliminate things such as computers, tablets, cell phones, smart watches, televisions and gaming devices. Stuff you need for cooking, fobs to enter your house or your car, and other such technology devices are perfectly acceptable to continue using. The benefit comes from reducing and eliminating screen time on a regular basis so that you can stay focused on life itself and all that life has to offer. These breaks are excellent at helping you eliminate technology addictions and reclaim your time.

10. Clean Up Social Media

We often spend a great deal of time on social media. A good idea is actually to clean up your social media. On a regular basis, you should unfollow pages and groups you don't like, eliminate friends you do not enjoy having around, and clean up your pages so that they are more favorable to you.

Spending a significant amount of time-consuming information on social media means that you are exposing yourself to a volatile environment. However, you do have a degree of control over what you see and who you see online, which means that you have the opportunity to make it a more favorable environment for yourself. You should take time regularly to clean up your social media accounts so that they remain as positive as possible. That way, any time you spend on your social media accounts will be positive and practical.

11. Morning Routines

There are many pieces of information floating around about what makes an effective morning routine, but something to consider is what <u>doesn't</u> make a solid morning routine. Ineffective morning routines are virtually any routine that has too many things going on. In the morning, you likely have two goals: wake up in a positive mood and acquire enough energy to tackle the day ahead of you. Every single activity you do in the morning should fulfill these needs. If you find you are partaking in any morning routine activities that are not beneficial to you, then you should remove these events from your routine. It is not always necessary to replace them with anything else; you merely need to create a morning routine that serves you.

Many times, you will read that a routine should be an absolute length or include some aspects to be productive. The reality is that you can have a productive 10-minute morning routine, or you can have a productive 45 minute or more extended morning routine. The amount of time it takes, you to complete your routine and what is specifically involved is unique to you, and it should only consist of things that help you feel energized and confident about your day. If it just takes you five minutes to do that, great! If it makes you an hour to do this, that's completely fine as thoroughly.

12. Other Routines

There are many different routines you partake in throughout your day, as well. In many instances, we establish a method and never revisit it to see if we are using the most efficient manner available to us. It is a good idea to visit routine tasks you do on a regular basis to make them more efficient and effective, if possible.

For example, perhaps you always take the same way to work, but due to the installation of new traffic measures, there is a new route that would be quicker or easier for you to choose. However, perhaps because you never revisit your routine, you are still making the long way to work. Now would be an excellent time to visit this method and change it. Alternatively, perhaps you always do the dishes by washing and thoroughly drying and then rewashing them, when you can directly learn to stack them more efficiently so that you do not have to wipe them in between. In this case, you can only stack them better, or wash them more frequently, and make the task significantly more comfortable.

It is a good idea to look at anything you do daily without thinking about it and find any ways you might be able to enhance these routines to become more efficient and efficient. The better these methods serve you, the more relaxed you are going to be able to get through them and spend the rest of your free time enjoying life.

Your time is valuable, and a significant part of minimalism is recognizing the value in your time and spending it wisely. Many people place an enormous amount of money and material objects and fail to realize how negatively this all affects their time, which tends to be more valuable than money or substantial items. Minimalism is all about learning to replace your value on time and spend it in a way that serves you. You want to spend your time in a way that is effective and efficient so that you can gain the most enjoyment and positivity out of life possible.

13. Forget About Perfection

Something vital for you to learn is that you need to forget about perfection. Perfection is something that adds stress to our lives and makes it harder for us to enjoy life itself. We spend so much time trying to get everything right that we fail to spend time doing. Applying minimalist skills to your life means that you eliminate the need to be perfect and you learn how just to be. Of course, it doesn't say that you don't need to give it you're all. Instead, it means that you just give it your best and then you appreciate it.

Forgetting about perfection and focusing on doing means that you accomplish more in your life. When you let go of your attachment towards doing things entirely, you give yourself the freedom to feel more confident and happier with what you do accomplish when you try your best. You take away the constant feelings of inadequacy and incompetence, and you give yourself the opportunity to feel powerful and confident.

14. Do What You Love

You should practice investing time in doing something you love every single day. Waiting to enjoy time doing what you love is never beneficial, and it can reduce your quality of life. Doing something you like every single day gives you the opportunity to enjoy your life every single day, as well. You don't have to do something major, but you should do at least one thing per day to help you enjoy life more.

Some ideas of what you might do include: cooking or eating a meal that you love, going on a scenic walk somewhere you like, practicing a hobby or activity that you enjoy, or doing any other number of smaller things you want. You might also do something more significant, such as travel somewhere, take a new class, or do something more involved that you would want to do. There is no limit to what you can or can't do when you are doing what you love. Instead, only do it.

Also, you should learn to turn everything into something you enjoy more. You may not necessarily love everything, but you can certainly make it more enjoyable for you. For example, instead of just cleaning the dishes see if you can turn it into a game and make it more enjoyable. Or, instead of only sweeping the floors, set the broom into your make-shift microphone and have an at-home concert for one.

There are so many ways to turn everyday activities into ones that you love creatively; there is no reason to spend each day doing mundane things out of obligation.

15. Evaluate Your Schedule

Take some time to think about your schedule. Do you enjoy everything that is on it? Is it fulfilling you or making you feel happy? If you are not satisfied with your program, you need to adjust it to make it fit your needs. If it is overwhelming, find a way to tone it down and make more time for relaxation and peace. If your schedule is underwhelming, find some new activities that you can add to your regular schedule. Sometimes you may not have an overwhelming or underwhelming plan but rather very little of what's on it lights you up and makes you feel happy. If this is the case, you should find a way to add more to it that will bring you joy and make you love your life even more.

Your schedule can be a fantastic tool to help you experience more joy, or it can be a dangerous device that destroys your happiness. If you can manage your schedule wisely, you can have an incredible selection of plans set up that allow you to control your responsibilities and enjoy life itself. Ideally, you want to learn how you can balance your schedule in this harmonious way.

16. Explore the World

Exploring the world is a valuable means to add happiness, joy, and education into your daily life. Of course, most of us can't pack up and explore the world every single day or at the drop of a hat. However, living a more minimalistic lifestyle means that you have much more freedom to explore your way. With fewer expenses and more time, you can do whatever you want for the most part. You should take advantage of this by exploring the world.

You can explore the world around you, or you can travel out and explore elsewhere in the world. There is no limit or rules on what you can or should do when you are investigating. Directly go where your heart takes you. Each new exploration will bring you so much value and knowledge in your life, and most will bring about a broad sense of joy and happiness that enrich your life in ways that other learning resources only cannot.

The world is a brilliant place, and one of the joys of being a minimalist is that it becomes easier for you to explore and enjoy the world. Whether you are hiking, camping, flying, traveling by train, going across countries, or staying in your backyard, nothing beats exploring the world around you and getting to know it better.

17. Do Something New

Have you ever felt like time just melts away? One moment it's a blistering hot summer day, and you're sipping an iced drink, and the next moment it's a cold winter day three years later, and you're in the same spot, only drinking a hot beverage? Research suggests that time melts away because we are continually doing the same thing every day. Average individuals wake up, go to work, spend eight hours working, come home, relax, go to bed, and then do it all over again.

As a minimalist, you have the perfect opportunity to break this cycle and lead a life where every day is precious and diverse from the last, and each one is memorable and serves a purpose in allowing you to be a happier version of yourself. All you have to do is practice doing something new each day. Or at the very least, something new each week. You can do something as small as making an original recipe or driving a new route, or something more substantial like traveling to a new place or picking up a new hobby. Doing something new breaks up the mundane and puts some pep back into your routine. It makes each day stand out and unique from the last, and from the rest that is yet to come. It makes life exciting and keeps sparks. Time will slow down a little as each day won't melt into one another, making life difficult for you to enjoy overall. It is indeed an excellent opportunity to retake control over your life and start living one that you love, to the fullest.

18. Release Ties

How many times are you holding onto because you are too scared to let go? Or, because giving go would be too inconvenient. These relations may be to friends, objects, places, or any other number of things that you hold onto in life. Relationships are common, and you will never get rid of your tendency to create relations towards stuff in your life. However, it is essential that you regularly weed your life and rid yourself of the relationship that does not serve you or bring you joy in life.

Releasing ties gives you the opportunity to let go of the past and open yourself up to bigger and better things. You are granted the chance to refresh yourself and open up space in your life. You stop feeling guilty or even ashamed around specific people, places, or things and you start feeling free once again.

It can be hard to release ties, primarily when we have invested a significant amount of time, emotion, or energy into keeping them. However, the value you can gain from freeing yourself from those ties is immeasurable. Think about how much more devastated you will be if you invest even more time, emotion and energy into something that will serve you. Eventually, it is going to filter out, either because it naturally ends or because you just can't take any more. It is better to cut ties when you are in control and have the power to do so on your own.

19. Fall in Love with Yourself

You are the only person you have to live every single day of your life with. Others will come and go. Some will be there for a long time, but none will ever be immediately by your side for every day of every minute of your life. Only you will be. If you don't take the time to fall in love with yourself and create a relationship with yourself that you love, you aren't going to have much fun in life.

Falling in love with yourself is essential, and you should invest in it every day. Think of it like a marriage: if you don't spend the time to work on it, it will fall apart. Of course, there are going to be ups and downs, but you should always take the time to be gentle with yourself and love yourself as you would your spouse. Only, enjoy yourself even more. You are valuable, and you are worth it, and as a result, you should always find the time to fall in love with yourself daily. You deserve it.

20. Evaluate Your In-Home Entertainment

How much time do you spend entertaining in your home? For many of us, we don't consider on a daily or even a weekly basis. If this is true for you, then you need to take some time sorting through your stuff and eliminating what you don't need. There is no need to hold on to things for entertaining guests if you rarely have guests over. This only requires you to use up storage space for something you don't need, which goes against the fundamental values of minimalism. It is time for you to get honest with yourself about your entertainment schedule and reduce your entertaining items to reflect that program.

Your daily life can be significantly affected by minimalism. We frequently find ourselves living an everyday life that is uncomfortable, unfulfilling, and often filled with unnecessary activities. If you want to make a change in your life, you need to embrace minimalist values beyond just your physical belongings. You need to be willing to apply them elsewhere in life too so that you can free yourself from all that does not serve you or bring you joy and lead a life that does.

Chapter 10:
How to Maintain Your
Minimalist Life

Maintaining your minimalist lifestyle is equally as important as adopting it, and it is the harder part of being a minimalist. Eventually it will become more comfortable, but in the beginning, this will be the hardest part.

See, in the very beginning when you are getting rid of everything and seeing "the light at the end of the tunnel" it can be straightforward to truck on as a minimalist. The cathartic effect of seeing clear spaces in your home and your life is so satisfying that you almost get onto a sort of "minimalist high" that feels so good. But then one day you are going to run into an experience where you are going to feel compelled to purchase something you don't need, or you are going to come home and realize that you have brought home several items you didn't need. And you might feel like you are back to square one. This is because the honeymoon phase of the new lifestyle has changed.

This honeymoon phase exists with any new lifestyle. It is often what people refer to when they say "the novelty wore off." But, if you want to be a true minimalist, you need to work past the dropping off of the honeymoon phase and continue working towards being a minimalist. Otherwise, you are going to end up back in the same place you were when you started: either staring at a room full of clutter saying "I can't do this anymore" or staring at a jam-packed schedule that is full of unhappy appointments saying "I can't do this anymore." It will not serve you to go back on what you have created up until this point.

Setbacks are expected, and difficult times are going to happen. Every new lifestyle comes with a point where your honeymoon phase ends and the real settling in begins. When this happens to you depends on you, how excited you were to change your lifestyle, and what the lifestyle change meant to you. However, you should realize that it is going to happen. When it does, you are going to want to be equipped with knowledge on how to handle the setbacks that may occur.

Maintaining your minimalist lifestyle will become difficult for a short period. However, eventually you will push through that time, and it will become easier. Soon enough it will become second nature to you, and you will realize that the value you gain from the lifestyle outweighs the minor inconveniences you may experience in your daily life from time to time. The following tips will help walk you through this maintenance period and teach you how you can make your minimalist lifestyle stay for good.

1. Take a Shopping Hiatus

It is essential to know when to stop shopping. Once you have everything you need, there is rarely a need to acquire more. Such an action would be a consumerism lifestyle, not a minimalist lifestyle. If you want to maintain your minimalism, you need to take regular shopping hiatuses. Only purchase what you need, and refrain from buying anything more. You can even take it one step further and make total breaks every now and again. For example, try not spending money for an entire week, not even on food. Most people can quickly do this by consuming the food that they have built up in their fridge.

Shopping hiatuses remind us to stop spending what we don't need to spend and to instead invest in what matters. Additionally, they teach us to find joy elsewhere in life, such as where money can't buy happiness. There are many things you can do instead of spending money; it merely takes some time to discover what and how. With each shopping hiatus, you will become even better at lasting longer and still having a fulfilling life for the duration of your break. Consider it a minimalist game!

2. Quality over Quantity

When you are shopping, always make sure that you look for quality over quantity. There is no value in having a significant number of things that do not hold any value. Instead, you want to invest in things that will bring value to your life. Clothing that lasts, cleaning products that work well and furniture that lasts are all the better than having a significant number of items that fall apart or don't do their intended job.

One of the many pitfalls of the consumerism lifestyle is the "I'll just buy it cheap now so that I can buy more items and then I will replace it with something better later." Ever notice how later never comes, and items often get replaced with more cheap items? That is because they shop with this mindset every single time. Instead, go in with the intention of coming out with nothing except the best that will fit exactly what you need. If you need a couch find the one that brings you joy, serves its purpose well, and will last for a long time. That way, you don't see yourself buying another couch in a few months or a year because you invested in one that fell apart fresh off the delivery truck.

3. Ditch Sales

Sales are a high consumerism environment that you need to learn to ditch as a minimalist. Sales encourage us to spend more money than we wanted to and bring home more items than we meant to. They quickly lead to us having a significant amount of clutter overrunning our house once again. As a minimalist, you need to ditch the sales.

The only time you should attend a sale is if you have something concrete you are looking for and you know that it will be on sale and you have the discipline to go in, get that, and leave. If you don't, you should not go. Going in and coming out with more than you needed or wanted is dangerous, as it leads you back to the consumerist lifestyle. It is best to ditch the sales altogether. At the very least, never go into one without a clear goal and plan.

4. Focus on Your Mindset

Your mindset is the most significant player when it comes to succeeding in any lifestyle. When you want to maintain a minimalist lifestyle, you need always to be thinking like a minimalist. Look for ways to reduce the number of harmful attachments and ties you have in your life and ways to enhance the number of positive ones. This will help you feel better about yourself and your life on an ongoing basis. Your mindset is always the most significant player in whether you will succeed in what you have set out to accomplish.

Remember how you were encouraged to get clear on why you wanted to be a minimalist in chapter one? Having these written down makes it easy for you to work on your mindset on a regular basis and keep yourself on track with the lifestyle you desire to live. Eventually, it will become second nature, and you won't even have to think twice: you will just be a minimalist by nature. Until then, always stay very focused on your mindset and maintaining it to be a minimalist.

5. Continue Practicing

Minimalism is a journey, as you have already learned. You always have to be willing to continue practicing. There are going to be times where you have a hiccup, and you spend more than you should have, or you bring home more than you intended. You will still experience buyer's remorse and wish you would have spent your money on something different. You live, and you learn, minimalism won't take you away from that rule of life. However, the most significant point is that you keep practicing. The more you practice being a minimalist and staying balanced in your lifestyle, the more success you are going to have. Nothing comes easy, not even if you make it come naturally to you.

6. Find Inspiration

Keeping your ability to stay functional as a minimalist means that you need to learn how you can find inspiration to keep on track with your lifestyle. Inspiration can be found in many places, from social media to magazines and even in the local minimalist community.

Inspiration can come in many forms. You might feel inspired to reduce the amount of stuff you use, encouraged to find new ways to use things you have, and feel encouraged to live life more comfortable. Maybe you will feel inspired to spend your free time in a better way that allows you to enjoy your life. Finding inspiration is an essential way for you to continue being happy, enjoying life, and living as a functional and successful minimalist.

7. Make Minimalist Friends

As a minimalist, it can be hard to spend time with consumers. While you likely don't judge other people for their way of living, it can be challenging to pay life the way you want to spend it. A lot of time consumers do not have enough money to live life the same way that minimalists do. They may also want to spend time shopping and otherwise spend money on things that don't mean as much to you anymore. Spending time with people like that can be hard.

While you don't need to let go of your consumer friends, it can be beneficial to acquire new minimalist friends. You want to find people who live life with the same values as you and who can help you along your minimalist path. Being friends with other minimalists allows you the opportunity to be friends with those who can help you advance along your route, who recognize your values and understand your motives, and who can enjoy life with you in a way that enriches your life.

8. Live Life to the Fullest

One of the biggest reasons why people become a minimalist is so that they can live life to the fullest without the holdbacks of material belongings and the expenses they bring about. You just can't become a minimalist if you aren't going to live your life to the fullest. The best way is to make sure that you are embracing every single day and getting the maximum pleasure out of it that you possibly can. The more you enjoy each day, the more satisfying and fulfilling your lifelong journey is going to be.

Life is about joy, entertainment, satisfaction, growth, learning, exploring, and so much more. It is crucial that you learn to take advantage of these qualities and infuse them into your daily life. The more you enjoy your life, the more you are going to enjoy who you are and feel fulfilled in your life.

As well, people who genuinely enjoy life are less likely to stress shop, and therefore they will be more likely to continue enjoying life to the fullest. It can be easy to feel stressed out and head out to the stores to fix any ailment they are grappling with what is known as "retail therapy." The reality is, however, retail therapy is more damaging than positive. Retail treatment leads to you spending money you didn't intend to, which can lead to you having less pay for what you need and therefore becoming further stressed out. If you want to make a change, you need to learn to stop using retail therapy as your go-to source, which keeping your stress in check. Living life to the fullest can help you do just that.

Maintaining your minimalist lifestyle is not as hard as it may seem. There are many natural ways that you can keep your lifestyle in check without ever feeling as though you are lacking or you have less than others. In fact, the wealthiest people are those who feel genuinely satisfied with what they already have in life. Those who want more will probably never find it through purchasing more and more belongings. The journey inside is the only way to find pure satisfaction and fulfillment, so when you learn to see that, then all of your material possession suddenly loses such a grand meaning in life. It becomes much easier to maintain your lifestyle, and in fact, it becomes so profoundly fulfilling that you will likely never think about living any other way ever again.

Remember, minimalism is a journey, and you are going to have ups and downs. You may still find yourself following old habits that you have developed for many years. That is okay and completely normal. Be gentle with yourself, learn from it, and find a way to bring yourself back into the world of minimalism. Eventually, it will become much more accessible to stop impulse shopping before it even begins, allowing you to maintain your minimalist lifestyle effortlessly honestly.

Conclusion

Thank you again for purchasing this book!

I hope this book was able to help you to adopt a minimalist lifestyle.

The next step is to follow the discussed strategies in this book.

Manuscript 2

Declutter Your Home

———— ༺༻ ————

The Ultimate Guide to Simplify and Organize Your Home

Chloe S

Introduction

I want to thank you and congratulate you for Purchasing the book, *"Declutter Your Home."*

This book contains *proven* steps and painless strategies about how to declutter your home.

Have you ever imagined how much junk you have lying around the house? What happened that time when a friend called you and said she'd drop by in a *few minutes?* Yikes! You immediately went into a panic, as you glanced at the shelves in your wall unit and noticed all the dust. Of course, you didn't have time to pick up very little knick-knack and dust underneath. What's more, you have a wealth of appliances occupying space on your kitchen counters because there's no more room in the cabinets to store them. There's barely enough space to prepare a little snack for your guest! Besides, everybody *always goes into the kitchen*. And yours is a horror show! *(Gasp!)*

Well, it is sad that most of us even have more than a little. Before you became enlightened, you barely noticed the clutter anymore. It is as if it becomes "friendly clutter." The marketing mavens of the world have surreptitiously misled people into believing that material things can help fill their human needs for self-esteem and social status. At this point, you have come to realize that all of that clutter is just STUFF! According to polls conducted by the National Association of Professional Organizers, over 65 % of American people often have the feeling that their house is disorganized and cluttered. So, you aren't alone. Many others are like you. What the others may not know is the fact that clutter accumulation in the house is very detrimental to human health. In many instances, it is clutter that stirs up stress. You've reached that point now, haven't you? Rather than get out your frustrations at the gym, why not harness your energy toward a more productive task?

Because you have picked up this book, you have already come to the understanding that living a simple and uncluttered life is very attractive. Can you imagine how terrific it would feel if you could tell any unexpected guest "Oh, sure...come on over?" Can you imagine yourself feeling delighted about your visitor, rather than rush about stressed out about the condition of your house! You want your house to be a home, not a multi-room storage locker.

To make your "house makeover" permanent, it is crucial to debunk the myths promulgated by that notorious army of greedy marketing mavens.

Although your clutter only consists of material things, letting go isn't easy – believe it or not. Therefore, it is crucial to understand the psychological reasons for your attachment to your stuff. Once you are freed from all those items holding you back, you will undergo a personal transformation. Is it possible the decluttering can have such a grandiose outcome? Yes, it is! It is a feeling of exhilarated freedom and mental tranquility.

Thank you for downloading this book. You will benefit from it!

Chapter 1:
Congratulations!

Isn't that what is said when people graduate and embark on the journey toward a bright and prosperous future? What does that have to do with decluttering your home? A great deal. Decluttering is not merely a long and weary exercise meant to help you divest yourself of the unnecessary, unwanted and useless. It is a major step in *Self-Transformation!*

In a study by the *Association of Consumer Research*, Aaron Ahuvia and Nancy Wong proved that there is a negative relationship between life satisfaction and materialism. In fact, they took it one step further through the administration of standardized tests when results showed that "...high aspirations for income is <u>negatively</u> associated with life satisfaction." That is what is promulgated worldwide. Likewise, the clarion call of advertisers tells you that ownership is a sign of success, riches, and happiness. Clinical studies have proven that this is not true.

What!? Even wealth and the symbols of wealth won't deliver self-satisfaction?

Things, including money, are unrewarding in and of themselves.

Chapter 2:
Debunking the Clutter Myths

Your Personal Revelation

In your latest trip around your house, you noted all the clutter you've amassed over the years. It didn't help you feel satisfied; it led to stress. Did you feel overwhelmed too? Consider this real-life tale:

Sandi's Paths

Sandi's two friends from graduate school, Jenny, and Phil lived miles away from Sandi. One day, they were going to be in the area and thought they might stop by and visit her. Sandi, who had been feeling depressed welcomed the visit and invited them over.

With happy anticipation, they rang her bell.

Sandi met them with a very warm greeting and ushered them inside. Jenny and Phil were led up the hallway and into the living room. Much to their astonishment, the living room was full of boxes, and there were additional unpackaged items stacked up in piles. Gingerly, the visitors were led on paths around the stacks and directed toward the kitchen. It was the only place where there were three unoccupied chairs!

Furtively, Jenny and Phil exchanged worried glances. Feeling the need to rationalize her "collection," Sandi explained that she was reorganizing her things. Evidence of dust on the multitude of boxes told the tale that Sandi was procrastinating and sidetracking her worthy goal. She was no doubt feeling overwhelmed and became stuck in a rut, paralyzed by her negative emotions.

As you noted all the clutter in your home, did you have visions of a future like that? No doubt, you may have. That is why you're breaking into a new direction in life. Although it might be a tad frightening, you are courageously taking up the gauntlet to combat the problem head-on.

Shedding the Old Myths

Philosophers and teachers throughout time have traditionally rejected the lure of greed and materialism. With the current 21st century movement toward minimalism, people have started eschewing the myths that there would be a psychological benefit to an accumulation of things. Among the false beliefs are:

- **Myth 1:** Self-Esteem can be attained through possessions.
- **Myth 2:** The esteem of others can be secured through ownership.
- **Myth 3:** Life is more convenient and easier if you conform to societal expectations.

- **Myth 4:** Security in oneself can be reinforced through materialism.
- **Myth 5:** Sentimental attachments give one a sense of emotional wellness.

Myth 1: Self-Esteem Can Be Attained through Possessions

In 1995, an elderly man was once interred along with his beloved Corvette. It was said of him that he "wanted to go out in style." Rather than being remembered for his winning personality, his caring, or his virtue, his friends, and others read his obituary and thought of him as the guy who was buried in his car!

As you watch TV or surf the Internet, you are pummeled with commercials and ads. When you walk through a large "big box" store, the glass windows are frightfully obscured with immense signs heralding "lower" prices or announcing specials. Once inside, you are bombarded with signs and sometimes even flashing lights. Standing displays block large portions of the aisles, which children knock over periodically.

There is, of course, one purpose to this barrage. To sell. Have you ever noticed what the sales profession calls their pitch? The "Call to Action." To achieve that, mighty promises are made. Most have to do with your self-image. You will be smarter than all the rest if you buy thus-and-so. You will feel better once you are the "proud owner" of a product. You will look better if you use this or that...terrific! Furthermore, the sales pitch adds: "Do it *Now!*" "Now" is a keyword of advertising. "Be the first to own..." is another catchphrase.

Today, there is such an emphasis on possessions and ownership that – indeed – people have been misled into considering objects necessary for their self-esteem. This can happen very easily, and it is human nature.

In his theory of motivation, the noted psychologist, Abraham Maslow, has indicated that every human being has set of needs. Self-esteem and the esteem of others are seen as some of the higher-level needs. One needs to find fulfillment in his or her esteem needs, and that will serve as a distinct motivation to grow as a person. What the advertisers have done is to imply that the possession of "stuff" will help you meet those needs and consider yourself a worthy person. That is quite a tall order for a material object. One can also realize a sense of self-fulfillment in the accumulation of things, so they say.

Have you ever noticed how huge corporations attempt to outdo the other? They try to buy out other companies, merge the two, or simply raid the lesser corporation for its monetary worth alone. Owners of such corporations do battle with each other also so that they can be perceived as the epitome in their respective fields. Don't you love it when billionaires fight?

Brief Exercise:

1. Make a list of all your positive qualities.
2. Made a list of all your negative characteristics.
3. Try to even out the list. That is, note that you put down more negative traits than positive ones. Spend some time thinking about your positive characteristics and list them.
4. Ask yourself the following question: Will owning that item or items help me feel better as a person?

Reflect on this quote from "The Little Prince" by Antoine de Saint-Exupery: "It is only with the heart that one can see rightly. What is essential is invisible to the eye."

Preliminary Solution:

Scribble a drawing of one room in your house. Notice how you left all the clutter out. No one wants to put their clutter on display, so you mentally eliminated it. Scan that room again noticing how it looks. Now create a visual picture of how you would *like* the room to look. Create a décor in your mind that you would want without the clutter. Once you've created that visual image, keep it in your mind as you begin the process of decluttering. Visual imagery is a powerful motivator.

Myth 2: The Esteem of Others Can Be Secured through Ownership

Today, people are often admired based on how many things they own. Surely, you've heard people utter with great majesty: "Oh! *I* have one of those!" Besides, take a look at written articles about achieving success. Virtually all of them indicate how many things the successful person owns. Because of that, you are expected to admire and respect them. Many fall into that trap.

In actuality, people read stories about successful entrepreneurs because they want to compete with them not have all the things they have. If that entrepreneur is successful, all you need do is mimic their formulas, and you too can be as rich, as happy, and as successful as they are. Concerning celebrities, the film director, Martin Scorsese said, "You get to love them. They don't know you. But you love them. But you love, I think, is what you imagine they are...they represent a dream. You lose yourself in these people." However, take a closer look. Those celebrities who have a truly unique style are admired because of their skills and personalities, not because of their wealth or how many things they own.

1. The Call to Conformity

    In modern society, the "Tyrants of Conformity" parade tempting images before you with the implication – either overt or implied – that you must act, dress, look, and own things to gain the esteem of others. Furthermore, you have been inculcated with the notion that ownership is necessary to reach a certain status in society. For example, you might hear someone say in astonishment: "What? You don't have the latest iPhone?" "Don't you have a riding lawnmower yet?"

    You are "supposed" to have a laptop, a cell phone, a flat screen TV, and, also, be trim and fit, muscular, wear a lot of stylish clothes, have a lot of hair, maintain certain hairstyles, and spend your morning routines trying to look like a model. *Why? So people will like you!* In contradiction to the call to conformity, have you ever noticed that the visual images advertised show home interiors with NO electronic gadgets strewn about here and there? Obviously, there is something inherently wrong with the belief that ownership makes the person.

There are odd behaviors, also, that you are expected to follow. When you travel the aisles in a grocery store, somehow, you are expected to speak in subdued tones. Anyone deviating will attract undue attention. (Children love to do that, don't they?) If you work in a corporate office, you are supposed to wear skimpy dresses or slim, trim suits – a different one each day of the week. Your wardrobe costs a fortune. If you don't adhere to the tenets of conformity, the prevailing attitude is that you won't be liked. There are a countless number of successful entrepreneurs who don't conform. They look like ordinary people without a lot of trappings and paraphernalia. That's what makes them interesting. They are not conformists; they are unique.

2. The False Goal of Conformity

   For years, you have been misled to believe that conformist behavior leads to the respect and esteem of others. To meet your objectives in life, you *simply* must follow the precepts of practices according to the overlords of society. Really?

   The real outcome of conformity is vastly different than the belief that you will attain the esteem of others. As you look upon a crowd of conformists, you don't see any significant differences. No one stands out. Do you want to be a nameless face in a sea of other nameless faces? Of course not!

3. Conformity ≠ Esteem of Others. So, how do you achieve the esteem of others? You don't! The esteem of others is not achieved. It is freely given, and you cannot control it. Some say that you "earn" the esteem of others. That belief is faulty. It is not up to you to "earn" or "strive" toward the esteem of others. It is a human failing to try to attain the attention of others. The esteem of others flows from who you are, and not what you own. There once was a character who appeared in cartoons during the

1930s. He famously said: "I am what I am and that's all that I am. I'm Popeye, the sailor man."

4. Irrational Beliefs

   People who crave the esteem of others subscribe to the code that it is necessary the everyone approves of them. They believe that unhappiness is caused by someone or something outside of oneself. Not to be undone, others believe that every unhappy event that befalls them is caused by themselves. Those folks are the "It's my fault" mob. You've seen that most vividly in teenagers. An unhappy girl feels that owning designer jeans and designer bags will make everyone like her more. Perhaps she is liked but doesn't even know it. It is also true that no one is liked by virtually everyone!

Myth 3: Life Is More Convenient and Easier If You Conform to Societal Expectations

Many commercials and ads display electronic devices that supposedly take the place of many other devices. Your cell phone now seems to do everything for you except put gas in your car! Devices pop up in your kitchen or living room that take commands. The sales pitch crows that you no longer need a lot of devices now – each for a specific purpose – all you need now is one device can do everything! The word *convenient* is added to all the jingles! How many times have you heard someone cry out in frustration: "Where is _____? *My whole life is in that* _____*!*" Wow! Your life is locked up in a memory chip! How convenient is that? "No, wait!" the advertisers say, "Now we have a device that tells you where your other device is!" So, now you have one device with everything on it, and a second device that tells you where it is! Each device comes with adapter cables or plugs for recharging. Then there's an extra cable in case you want to plug anything into your cigarette lighter. Now, you have up to five pieces of clutter!

Not to be outdone, clever entrepreneurs have designed containers in which to keep your things. It's a "convenient" way to avoid decluttering too!

While some people think that the best option is to get containers in which to pack these things, the truth is that it helps you avoid the most painful thing of all! Getting rid of the clutter. You can easily stack up containers on the top of your closet shelf until they reach the ceiling, but you'll have to deal with the items inside someday. The easiest way to get rid of this stuff is to make it a game to get rid of at least ten things each day. This means that, if you have emotional attachments to things but know you don't have room to store them, you can find creative ways to preserve memories without necessarily keeping all the items. Some of the things that create clutter include photos, souvenirs, and albums – digital and otherwise. Other targets include small appliances and utensils you no longer use, old makeup kits, excess bedding, and vestiges from old technologies such as DVDs, cassettes, and CDs among others.

The things that we love to keep are not self-sufficient! Those things require that you dust them, care for them, maintain them, pack, unpack and rearrange them. They need more attention than pets! If their things that you don't need, spending your time and effort cleaning them is a waste. Hard as it is to let go of things you've spent money on, it's even harder to waste energy and time storing stuff that you don't care about. Most of the time you run out of places to store everything.

The truth of the matter is that convenience doesn't justify keeping clutter in the house. Therefore, if what you have is junk, unnecessary duplicates, tattered or even broken items, you have to get rid of them.

The Legend of King Midas

In the sixth century, the legend of King Midas was born. He was the King of Phrygia in Asia Minor. He loved his luxury, and most of all loved gold. King Midas loved his things, but especially gold – lots of it. Soon he was noted, not for who he was as a person, but for his wealth. When Dionysius, the god of wine visited him, he offered Midas a wish. Because gold attracted so many powerful and influential people, Midas wished that everything he touched would turn into gold. Predictably, his food and drink turned into gold. Even his beloved daughter was converted into a golden statue. The fate of craving for the esteem of others is starvation, the ultimate loss of any chance to obtain the esteem of others.

According to Tsang et al. in the journal *Personality and Individual Differences*, "Materialism has been consistently related to lower levels of life satisfaction." In the years of the latter twentieth century and the twenty-first century, materialism has come to symbolize a social category. You have all heard the phrases: the "have's" and the "have-not's." This focus on ownership increases paranoid fears ("I might get robbed!) That certainly isn't satisfying. Take a look at poor Sadie's story:

Sadie's Little House

Sadie lived in a quaint little brick house in the country. She had many precious items on the multitudinous shelves there – golden figurines, tea sets of pure silver, ancient gold coins, Japanese Netsuke figurines, and the like. She enjoyed the adulation of neighbors and reveled in taking them on trips to her home, which she called a "museum." Her life was easy and convenient. Sadie had two children, who moved out and had their own families. They lived quite a distance from Sadie, as they weren't very fond of her. After all, they spent most of their young years forbidden to "touch" any of her precious things. As she grew older, the children who had children of their own did occasionally visit but had a secret agenda. They were hoping to ascertain what was in Sadie's will.

When Sadie died, her children and grandchildren dutifully attended the funeral. Her son arrived in a pickup truck, and her daughter had a U-Haul. Toward the end of the funeral, Sadie's son left in his truck with his family. He was followed shortly after that by Sadie's daughter.

On the street in front of Sadie's house, her son parked and began raiding the house. So did her daughter. In the middle of the street, a heated argument broke out between them. "But Mom promised me her rings and gold jewelry!" squealed her daughter. Then her brother bellowed: "I'm the first-born, and am entitled to whatever I want!"

In the meantime, the grandchildren ran in and out of the house toting as many objects as they could carry. A crowd gathered, and

*the police were called to quell the
disturbance.*

The above is a true story, including the truck, the U-Haul, and trained grandchildren! Perhaps you have heard other stories like that too.

Unfortunately, poor Sadie felt that others would only care about her if she could entertain them with her many precious things. People will like you for who you are as a person.

 Preliminary Solution (more to follow):

When you reflect on someone you like, ask yourself if the many conveniences their goods provided are the foundation for your fondness. When you think of someone you dislike, ask yourself if the lack of convenience in their lifestyle is the foundation for your negative feelings. The answer is a resounding "No!"

Now, when you think about someone who has an expensive foreign car with a chauffeur and lives in what is dubbed a "mini-mansion," do you think about their personalities? No! Years from now, if someone asks you about that person with expensive items and an easy life, you nearly always say: "Oh! He had a _____ and life was so much easier for him." One hounding follow-up question remains: "Does the convenience of ownership mean he or she is esteemed?"

It is usually the person who has a *less* convenient life who is more admired.

Myth 4: Security in Oneself can be Reinforced through Materialism.

According to some of the ancient philosophies, "materialism" is a firm conviction that nothing exists except matter and its movements. Many people you know go from one day to the next in a humdrum pace to maintain their standard of living, raise families, and simply survive. Since the Industrial Revolution, one's job has been the foundation for survival. It has become the motivation to work. In some cultures, citizens live to work, rather than work to live. The worship of the ever-growing desire for higher-paying jobs has been nominated as one's goal in life. According to M. L. Richins et al., "An important cause of increasing work and declining leisure among people is their materialistic values."

When you see your baby, you marvel at the wonder and awe he demonstrates toward others and the environment. When he looks out the window, he is wide-eyed when he sees a bird land on a branch outside. When you make a funny face, he giggles. When you pick him up and cuddle him, he feels delighted. When you feed him, he is content and happy. Family and friends give him toys, which he touches and caresses. However, he never asks for more. He loves you, and you cannot help but respond with love. Love is not material, yet it is what he needs most to survive.

As your child grows, however, suddenly he feels the need for things. Objects such as cell phones, computer tablets, video and music-related devices tend to bring him a sense of security. Meals, a warm house, and clothing are no longer sufficient. By the time your children reach adolescence, their rooms are so cluttered with objects that there's barely little space left for sleeping! You used to say "He outgrew his clothes." Now you can say, "His room outgrew him!"

In the process of self-examination, you discover that security seems to have become associated, not only with the necessities of physical survival but also with *things*.

What happened?

According to Hyunji Kim et al., this is called "personal relative deprivation." That means that people assess their feelings of a security relative to others. The most astounding result of Kim's five studies showed that absolute household income and ownership had much more to do with the ***desire*** for financial success and power than security. There is an undercurrent of fear involved in detaching yourself from things you feel are needed to give you a sense of security. Some possessions, of course, are necessary for human survival and to provide a sense of physical security. However, things will never provide psychological security. That kind of security comes from within.

Your self-image and sense of security within yourself depends on you, not what you own. Your esteem needs are fulfilled by your behaviors. Your need for love relies on others. You need to reach a level of self-actualization is accomplished through your values and attitudes. It takes great courage to move ahead in life when the most important elements of life depend upon your personality and spirit, not the material possessions you have.

Preliminary Solution (more to follow):

Mentally create this mindset – Freedom!

The sooner you get started on detaching yourself from material possessions, the sooner you will realize that there are other priorities such as placing more importance on experiences. At this point, you will have a strong sense of lightness. You will feel more secure knowing that you are more valuable than your things. It is like putting down all the load that you have been carrying for a very long time. You can channel your energy into people, family, friends, and experiences. Imagine scenes of enjoyment. Picture meaningful interactions with people you care about.

Myth 5: Sentimental Attachments Give One a Sense of Emotional Wellness

Yes! The photos. Is your cell phone exploding with them? Has anybody ever told you they want to show you a photo? Then they pick up their cell phone and flick through image after image until they find it. (In the meantime, you check your watch.) Before the cell phones, there were the notorious photo albums. Every trip you ever took, every family event, every attractive scene which looks like the work of a professional photographer is in those albums. What about the gifts? When Millie was seventy-years-old, she had lovely presents that her family and friends gave her on the holidays throughout the years. If someone remarked about her old jacket, Millie would surprisingly comment: "Oh, that's Sue's jacket." Well, it wasn't "Sue's jacket" at all; it was the jacket Sue gave her many moons ago! Millie couldn't bear to part with it because Sue was her favorite niece. Whenever she took new visitors for a little house tour, she always identified many of her possessions by the names of the people who gave them to her. "Aunt Camille's candy dish...Larry's vase...Maggie's chime clock..." Of course, that left visitors very puzzled.

In your heart of hearts, do you silently do that too? Is it from a fear of forgetting the past that creates the need to keep so many things? What is truly important from your past is how others have affected you and how you affect them. It is pleasant to reflect upon the warmth others have shared with you. Most of the people you have met have changed you in some way. It is what is in your heart and your memory that you cherish. It does not depend upon "reminder objects."

Many cultures and even religions throughout the centuries have placed value on the memories of their ancestors from the last generation. In Old Japan, they remembered their parents by carving soapstone statuettes of them. The people didn't save any other mementos. No doubt, you have the seen the simplistic style of their homes – free from clutter and trappings.

Preliminary Solution (more to follow):

The trick to becoming clutter-free is to think of it as a mental or spiritual exercise in which you shed the shackles of becoming a slave to your memories and the STUFF that those mementos entail. The sentiment exists in memory. The physical thing once enjoyed, is no longer relevant. Your past is derived from the experience of the warmth and caring of others and the love you have for them. Love is not a physical thing.

Chapter 3:
How to Start Decluttering

The most challenging thing of all is the start. What makes that so difficult is the feeling of being overwhelmed. That's normal. However, do you wait for the ideal time? The ideal time is *now*.

A series of transitions characterize every life. Decluttering represents a transition from what you were to what you will become. Transitional periods are unsettling. Your greatest need during this time is to find simple and painless ways to put things in the right order even in the most unfavorable conditions. The best way to do this is to pay close attention to the clutter that causes you the most frustration.

Initial exercise #1: Clutter Patrol!

1. *In your home, go from one room to the other.*
2. *Select the room that has the least amount of clutter.*
3. *Make a note of the time.*

4. Put all objects that do not belong in that room back into their rightful places.   Don't examine or scrutinize the contents of drawers or closets. That comes later in the process.

5. Move into the next least cluttered room. Do the same.

6. Continue to move from one room to the next, putting your stuff into the proper rooms. There will still be clutter leftover.

7. Take a look at your watch and make a note of how long this exercise took you. That will give you an idea of how serious your situation is.

Accept the fact that this is going to involve work...unpaid work! Make a firm commitment to pursue the task until you are finished.

Initial Exercise #2: A Family Affair

1. Schedule a family meeting.

2. Announce that you intend to embark on the project of decluttering your home, and indicate that it will continue for quite some time.

3. *Children from the age of ten and up wonder if that means you will be entering their rooms. Inform them that you will. If they offer many objections, enlist their help and teach them the method that you will adopt. Have them start with their rooms. Many will not keep up this activity, and you may need to remind them. Do so gently. If they don't cooperate with your efforts, enter their rooms and start with your chosen method. When you start, speak to them and start asking questions about the usefulness of one or two items. Watch! They will show up in a grand hurry, and you can thus get their help.*

Likewise, enlist the support of your spouse. You may have to cite certain trouble spots which he/she has left messy and cluttered. Tell your spouse that you don't want to decide upon which items to discard without his or her input.

Schedule and Organize

The first impediment to the deliberate act of decluttering your home is the emotional static it will create. Review the prior chapter and reflect upon the roots of materialism. Note that materialism is deleterious to your mental health and sense of well-being. Virtually all the clinical studies have confirmed that. The term "scheduling" seems innocuous enough, but it's a disciplinary practice. It's the first step. In the beginning, you may feel the need to make micro-movements. The micro-movements are composed of short sessions that can last up to 5 minutes each. You can also choose to declutter in 15-minute sessions or an hour a day. If it is possible, considering your work plan and effort, you might be able to do this as a 3-5 days marathon activity. Finally, another option is to choose to declutter each day of the week throughout the year. Believe it or not, most people increase their decluttering periods with time. You see, as they become more overwhelmed by the volume of stuff they've collected, it increases their motivation to continue. The growing frustration with the accumulation of things also serves as an incentive to complete this task quickly.

Designate a Purpose for Each Room

Every room should convey and mood. You may have some larger rooms that serve dual purposes, and you can separate one area from the other. For instance, you can designate the den as the place in which you would love to sit with your family and watch movies, television, chat, have fun and conduct recreational activities. Therefore, the proper mood to exude there is that of comfort and connection. In the laundry room, you might want to ensure that it is organized in such a manner to avoid any pile ups. The bathroom can have a spa-like surrounding to give a sweet, luxurious feeling. The master bedroom can have a romantic feel to it and yet be comfortable at the same time. Whichever room you are examining, ensure that you plan to organize it based on the function each room serves and the 'feel' you would like the room to have! That will help you decide to move related ancillary items from one room into the other. If you are going to study or read, you will need a comfortable chair or maybe a recliner, tall and small lamps, side tables (for snacks), and shelving for books. Perhaps your living room wall unit is crammed full of knick-knacks. If you plan on using that room a lot, your laptop might be appropriate to store on one of the shelves rather than knick-knacks. Why put it on the end table in your bedroom? Or carry it around with you. After all, you don't have to use your laptop in bed or at the dinner table. The Internet and your apps will survive without you! That way you can interact with your family in the dining room and spend time sleeping or romancing with your spouse in the bedroom.

Every room serves a function or two. That which is not in keeping with those functions is most likely clutter or misplaced. Ensure that your plans take comfort and livability into account while doing this.

Decide Where to Start

Most people often are tempted to begin their decluttering and organization from cabinets and drawers underneath the sink and in the hallway. While this is okay, it is even more effective and efficient to start with areas that are visible. Begin with a small task. Select the least used and least cluttered room first. Decluttering is traumatic because it means letting go. When you start with the least cluttered room, it will reduce the traumatic nature of your task. It's less threatening. When you conducted "Clutter Patrol" in the first preliminary exercise, you cleared out and returned your things to their rightful places. For instance, you identified all the things on the countertops, desktops, and tables that are not necessary or are not supposed to be located here and put them in the right rooms. However, you may have sadly discovered that there was "leftover stuff" for which there was no room. There were also larger objects that now occupy precious floor space. Those uncomfortable items will be relegated to the later stages of your plan. Now you can now move on to shelves, countertops, drawers, closets, and cabinets. Begin from the door and work clockwise throughout the room. Techniques for decluttering will be discussed next. Always ensure that you pay a close attention to one room at a time.

It is usually good to start with the least used room first, then move on to the next room that's used less often, and so on. The "Konmari" approach (Chapter 4) is somewhat different sequentially. Whichever method you choose depends on your personality and cleaning style.

Chapter 4:
Adopt a Technique

The Four-Box Technique

Find four boxes and a large magic marker. Bring them into the room you chose to start with. This means that you set out four boxes. One is for trash; the second is dedicated to selling, the next for donations and the last one is for stuff you plan on keeping. Label each box accordingly. Focus on visual items that are, those that are on the tops of tables and open shelves. Separate your things accordingly. Next, take your four boxes to the next room. You might find that you have already filled one of them, so you may need to start a new box to replace it.

As you put in one item after the other, ask yourself the following questions:

1. Is this object in good condition?

   If you have items in the house that are broken or tattered, then you need to throw them away. At this point, while decluttering, you do not need to dedicate things to fix if they're not important. If it is something that you want to fix, ensure that you put a timeline on when you will fix it and do it. If you're never going to get around to fixing it, toss it away.

2. If this item was broken, would I rebuy it?

   Most people have been victims of purchasing things they seldom or never use. Although you have already spent money on them, you may not need for them. Those are things you might resell or simply toss out.

3. Do I have one of these already?

   How many hair dryers do you need? How many tables do you need in the sitting area? All these questions and more are the things you need to take into consideration before decluttering seriously. You might think it's easy to get rid of all these duplicated items. It's not! Only some of items that aren't in bad condition may be sold at a garage sale. You can make some extra money on those, and you have a box for that. Other items have no resale value and deserve to be thrown out or donated.

4. Is this item worth saving?

There are many, many things that may look attractive or useful. That ratchet set is in an attractive case, and none are missing. However, if you bought it for a temporary usage, why save it? It might now sell well. Besides, do you have sufficient closet or shelf space for it? Probably not.

5. Have I used this item for the last six months?

   If you have gone for six months without using something, then there is a high probability that you won't ever need it! That is for resale or disposal. So toss it into the appropriate box.

6. Are these "just in case" items?

   When you are working on the first two rooms, you will discover a truth about your sense of security. As you categorize items, you may catch yourself thinking that you need to keep certain items "just in case" you need it for _____ someday. You may also note that these objects are usually inconsequential and inexpensive to buy. Rethink the issue and categorize accordingly.

7. Do these things fit into my future vision of life?

This is the most important question of them all. It is true that people often talk themselves into many things and even weasel their way around that question many times. However, it is you who needs to make a decision, keeping in mind your firm commitment to declutter. You have to weigh whether your choice is wise enough and in line with the vision you have for your family and home.

The truth of the matter is that no single reason can justify keeping clutter in the house. Therefore, if what you have are junky things, unnecessary duplicates, tattered or even broken items, decide to get rid of them either by selling them, donating them or discarding them.

Turn your house into a home! Ensure that the things you keep in your home are not only safe for you but also safe for your family, your guests, and your pets. People should feel comfortable and at ease whenever they are in your home. Keep your focus on your family and friends, rather than on material possessions that don't matter at all. Even your pets will demonstrate their comfort. Having friendlier surroundings has a tranquil effect on animals.

Be happy, healthy, safe and free. Do not allow stuff to control you. The only way to attain this is by living a clutter-free life forever.

The Time Segment Technique

During your house tour, you took note of the most cluttered room. Designate a time of about five minutes to a half-an-hour. Make up a "to-do list" for decluttering that room. There are some rooms that may require movement from section to section. It might be your office area or den. There are piles there, despite the fact that this is a digital world.

If you work mostly online, you are acutely aware of the junk files you've managed to create. Take that thirty minute time and clean up one folder after another. As each folder is finished, rename it, so you will recall which ones have been completed, and which ones still need attention. *Reboot your computer after you've completed each time segment. That will help you avoid computer slowdowns and frozen screens. Haven't you had the experience of hearing an apology from a clerk you've contacted to the effect that their computers are "slow today?" That's because they failed to clean up and reboot.

The Trash Bag Approach

This is a two-bag approach.

1. The Disposables
    As you rummage through your most cluttered room (including drawers and closets), you will come upon items that should be disposed of. Rather than piling up twenty bags of garbage, and trudging the load out to the end of your driveway on trash day, you can decide on placing one or two additional bags out in addition to your regular disposables. This, of course, is longer-term but will save the money of having to hire a junk service. Those can become very expensive.

2. The Giveaway's
    Research online and locate charity groups that will pick up items from you. Don't worry about whether it is a "legitimate" charity. Someone who needs your stuff will benefit.

3. The "Turnaround"

Because you have designated your disposables and giveaway items, you have changed your attitude. It is barely noticeable when it occurs but stands out after you've disposed of or gave away some of your stuff. You have learned how to let go of some material objects. What's more, you have noticed that your house now seems cleaner and neater. It was an enjoyable feeling, wasn't it? Try it again!

<u>Return to the rooms in your house.</u> Search inside your drawers. Ask yourself yet again why you decided to keep each of those items. You will quickly realize that parting with the other items make you feel better about yourself. It also strengthened your decision-making abilities. There are psychological rewards for this freeing behavior.

Again, decide whether or not each of the things in your drawers and closets is useful. Decide which ones bring you a sense of joy and are respected. Organize them neatly. Regarding clothing, ask yourself which ones deserve to hang up and which ones should be stored in drawers. Use the "roll-up" method of storing articles of clothing. Roll them up and stand them up vertically. Do not hesitate to leave space. Compliment yourself for having such a luxury.

The 12-12-12 Challenge

Make this challenge a part of your routine. This means that each day, you ensure that you locate 12 items to throw away, 12 to give up to charity and 12 to be taken back to their rightful position or into the rooms in your house. This challenge can be an enjoyable and exciting way to organize 36 items within a short duration. *Be sure to throw away, give away, or neatly store the items you have separated. *Do it fast before you change your mind!*

Repeat this process until there are empty areas in your drawers and on the tops of furniture.

The exercise of purging is uplifting. What's more, it will make it easier to clean and polish.

Exercise for Closet and Drawer Decluttering:
Start out by hanging all your clothes and jewelry in the reverse direction. Once you have worn them, put them back into the

148

closets and drawers in the right direction. Once 4-6 months elapse, if you have not used some things at all, those are the items you need to discard or sell at a garage sale. Don't save clothes that are ill-fitting. Don't save clothes that are torn with the intention that you will see them later. "Later" never happens.

Note: *Costume jewelry is valuable. * While you seldom may have worn the pin Aunt Jessie gave you, other people may find it quite attractive. If you don't want to sell it yourself or live in an area where costume jewelry is of little interest, you can always find resellers and dealers who anxiously crave it. Regardless of the distance involved, many of them will rush to your house to buy it!

The "Konmari" Method

This method is the most drastic of all and takes a lot of courage. If you have built up enough annoyance when you make your initial house tour, you will feel bound and determined to succeed with your decluttering process... If that matches your mindset, you will want to choose this approach.

1. Start with a room that is only moderately used. (No! Definitely not the kitchen!)
2. Choose to attack a closet, a cabinet or half of the drawers in a dresser.
3. Throw everything on the floor!
4. Neatly put back items that you use constantly. Don't include items that you feel you may or may not use in the next six months.
5. Grab three boxes. Label them "Trash," "Undecided," and "Give Away." Make decisions on your items, and place them in the boxes or back in the closet or drawers.
6. Move to the next closet, cabinet or set of drawers you want to tackle and do the same until you are done.
7. Continue to the next room which you use a little more often. Do up your three boxes as before.

Continue on to the next room until about half the rooms are categorized in the boxes and items of use are put away.

_____

_____

Halfway through your house, collect the items labeled "Trash" and put them into your garbage pails. Avoid second guessing.

_____

_____

8. Return to the room with the undecided boxes. Now it's time to decide! Be firm, and separate out that which really deserves to be trashed. Add that to your garbage pails. Pull out those things that are useful enough to give away, and move them into your "Give Away" box. If you really, really feel you need an item or two to keep, try to limit the number of saved items. Put them away neatly.

9. Now on those first few rooms, clear off the tops of your furniture. It's

a relief to see an empty table top, doesn't it? Take some time to rejoice in that feeling. It is good for your emotional well-being.

10. Clean the tops of the furniture and polish if appropriate. Now choose just a few items to place on top. The rest can go to charity or family and friends.

_____

_____

Now you are ready for the heavily used rooms. Those rooms are usually the kitchen, the mudroom, the home office and den if you have one. You will need to allocate more time to those rooms, obviously.

_____

_____

11. The Infamous Kitchen

a. A glance at your countertop. Assess the number of appliances you have stored on top, noting that some aren't used that often. However, before you can put them in your cabinets, you will have to create room for them there. Therefore, work the kitchen from the inside out – one cabinet at a time, starting with the lower cabinets. On the floor, separate the items into "always used," "used a few times a month," and "hardly ever used," and "used once or twice the past year." In two boxes separate the "hardly ever used" from the "used once or twice." Continue with the next lower cabinet and do the same. When you've finished with those boxes, temporarily put the "hardly ever used" and the "used once or twice in the past year" into another room.

b. Now, do you have room for those extra appliances cluttering your countertop? If so, decide as to whether or not you are going to save them. Then place the ones you want to keep in the spaces in your lower cabinets. Add the "always used" items and the "used once or twice" items.

c. Repeat the same procedure with your upper cabinets.

d. Return to the items you placed temporarily in the other room. Decide if you need them. They are the items marked "hardly ever used" and "used once or twice in the past year." Dispose of accordingly.

Note: By the time you reach this stage, you will be taking more drastic measures to get rid of unneeded items and reducing clutter.

12. The Mud Room

The mudroom is easier, despite the dirt and leaves that were dragged in from outside. Clean off the boots. Examine the jackets and coats and return them to their rightful places in the house, or throw into the laundry if needed. You will note that many items are duplicates. Perhaps some of ready for the trash. Clean the mudroom floor. That is a gratifying experience, and you will want to take the time to admire the results of your efforts.

13. The Home Office and Den

Yes, the office! That will take a while if you take a lot of work home from your job or if you have a side business. By the time you decide to declutter, you will realize that you've accumulated a lot of trinkets and containers stuffed with riff-raff. Those have little to do with your work, so start on them first. Desks should have a lot of space for your daily tasks. Some people have a lot of paper files stored in file cabinets or desk drawers. Once you go through them, you may discover that they contain many antiquated items that need to be thrown into the recycling bin. Sometimes entire files are no longer needed. Once you've cleared all that out, you may find out that you need far less space.

If you use a computer, that appropriately has a "desktop." If it's a jumble, return the misplaced folders into your documents or other specific areas you've designated. Next, go through the tedious task of straightening out your folders. Attack the moderately used folders first and trash the excesses. Then move to the moderately used folders and do the same. *Reboot your computer. Otherwise, your activity will slow your computer down to a crawl. Last to attack are your often-used and current files. You may need to create new file folders for those. By now, you'll have more room for them, if needed.

Note: Take some time to explore your hard disk file, open up your applications directory, and eliminate all those pesky extra games and the like that you aren't likely to use at all. Those are usually the ones that came with your computer when you purchased it.

For your den or that of your spouse, create a more utilitarian and fun area. Rearrange furniture to be conducive to the various functions it serves. Perhaps that might mean creating a little conversational area, or an area for watching TV and playing video games, or an area for music. Then there are areas to be designated for a dart board, a pool table or card table, for example. Different types of lighting will be needed in each of those areas. Maybe there's an extra lamp in another room of little use.

The "Drop Zone"

Every house has a "drop zone." That's a haphazardly selected area where your family puts the mail, where the children put their backpacks and leftover lunches, where you and your spouse dropped the car keys, and all sorts of junk. Designate a better area for those things. Of course, food items and backpacks don't belong in the "drop zone" at all. Encourage members of your family to cooperate in that effort. Most people would prefer to procrastinate that so that it might become an important family rule. Although it takes a little extra time and effort to execute that thankless task, it will eliminate early morning panics when someone can't find something. A cluttered "drop zone" is also the reason why some folks are late with invoices. (They get mixed up with the other clutter!) Invoices should be put in a designated area on your desk. If you have room, sometimes a card table or small tall table can serve the role of a "drop zone," rather than the kitchen table, by the way!

A word about containers

Some professionals recommend that you don't use containers in which to pack your clothes or cabinet items. Certain types might be helpful, although others might not be. Be very selective when you choose containers. There are some types of clothing hangers sold that hold a multitude of dresses or pants. They are not recommended for three reasons:

1. *You will be tempted to save far too many clothes.*
2. *Your clothing will get wrinkled up because everything is being crushed together.*
3. *The weight may be too heavy and the dowel in your closet will bend.*

Avoid the temptation of stacking plastic containers one on top of the other on your closet shelf. Eventually, you will need a step stool or even and ladder to reach the ones on top!

Installing smaller shelves in your closet may be very helpful. Most of those shelves aren't designed to hold a lot of excess sweaters, shirts, etc. That will help you trim down the amount of clothing you keep.

Containers that are stored in your bed are not recommended. They are inconvenient and gather dust bunnies!

Chapter 5:
Zen and the Art of Decluttering

If you walk through your cluttered house, it rattles the mind and creates stress. All of the clutter beckons out to you and creates busy thoughts in your mind like "Oh, I should finish this...I should put that away..." What's more, the multitude of colors that these objects have subtly creates chaos in your mind. If you're used to a cluttered house, the bombardment of your senses still has a very sneaky but insidious effect.

The Purpose and Function of Zen

Zen is a mental discipline that helps one focus on just one thing. In doing so, the mind is freed up from the business of things. Healing and tranquility take place. A quiet environment creates the mood for such an experience. A non-cluttered house silently creates an atmosphere that promotes feelings of peace and self-satisfaction. Quiet and restful surroundings make it so much easier to handle an onslaught of sudden noise. That, of course, occurs when your children or your spouse burst into the door after their day's work. It works for you, too, when you get home from your work. Imagine yourself coming home from your job and collapsing into an easy chair. Think about the relief you will feel escaping the constant tapping of keys at computer keyboards, the rustling created as co-workers wander the office floor and the sporadic, excited conversations. Sit for a while and listen to the quiet.

Look at an image of a Zen garden on the Internet. It just consists of a rock or two and parallels curved lines in the sand. Why is it so alluring? Take a look at a scenic picture of sands in the desert. Likewise, there is nothing there except the sun and the gentle rolling strokes caused by the wind sweeping over the sand. People love those photos. The quiet sensations they impart are mesmerizing.

The garden and the desert scene force you to silence the wanderings of your mind. For just a few moments, you reject those mental interruptions of thought to wonder in awe and amazement at the beauty of simplicity. Slowly, calmness replaces stress, and you begin to feel peaceful. You tap into the powers of your higher self – that precious part of you which throbs and undulates with the flow of life.

Mindfulness and the Zen Technique

Dr. Jon Kabat-Zinn went to the East to learn Zen meditation to control his chronic pain. He underwent all the stages of learning the Zen technique. It worked for him, so he introduced a Westernized version of it called Mindfulness Meditation. His techniques were thoroughly researched by clinicians and results were extremely successful. Mindfulness techniques were later applied to many fields.

Mindfulness consists of taking some time to focus upon the "here-and-now," by focusing upon breathing or upon a beautiful scene (the night sky, for example). Mental discipline occurs by ignoring the intrusion of stray thoughts that have a devious way of pummeling the conscious mind. This practice brings about a sense of peace and tranquility.

That is why an uncluttered home is important. It leaves space for you to focus mentally without being distracted by clutter. Your stuff won't be strewn about, beckoning to you to engage in non-related activities. You are stable and rooted in who you are as a person, rather than what you have to do.

The Art of Decluttering and Its Beneficial Effects upon the Brain

No doubt, you've heard the terms "left-brained" and "right-brained." The "left brain" is associated with conscious thoughts and logic. The "right brain" is associated with creativity and abstract thinking. Although those two parts of your brain don't function separately from each other, the analogy holds true. A certain area of your brain (the neocortex) handles more concrete concepts like logical problem-solving, daily tasks, and the discrete interpretations of events and experiences. It is a very busy area and requires processing information. Other areas called the "right brain" handle tasks like developing new ideas, creating new and unique solutions for old and recent dilemmas, and creative expressions of yourself that release pent-up energy and communicate to others without reliance upon voice.

The combination of your logical, concrete mind of thought and your creative, ingenious mind can yield many rewards.

Have you ever wondered how people developed innovative ideas and applied those creative ideas to the logic of the computer world? Those folks produce popular games, graphics programs that produce 3-D art out of a 2-D screen, new functional software, and the like. Likewise, art and music combine thought, structure and creativity.

Creativity combined with hands-on knowledge gave rise to Microsoft and Apple. True entrepreneurs rise to the top. They all thrive in uncluttered environments.

Conclusion

In this book, you have uncovered the truth and the psychological implications of consumerism. Because you felt shackled by too many products, you realized that you were looking for self-esteem and a fulfillment of your human needs in material things. After you discovered that no amount of material goods would help you become the person you wanted to be, you decided to divest yourself of your stuff and clutter. As you labored through the jungles of the paraphernalia that cluttered your house using your preferred tactical method of assault, you came to find what is most valuable to you without all the useless trappings.

Your house then became a home – a welcoming haven for you, your family and your friends. The atmosphere of your home has come to reflect you. You are unique and now live in an environment that radiates peace.

Manuscript 3

How to Clean Your House

— — — — — ❧❦❧ — — — — —

100 Easy Tips and Action Plan of Revolutionary Cleaning Mindset

Chloe S

Introduction

Consider this: Your time and how you spend it is basically your life. If your home and castle are not set up—organized—to support you in exploring your passions or recharging from your wild-and-crazy outside life, then you are wasting your life.

Who says the "dining room" space has to be a dining room if you never formally entertain? Why not make it a library, music room, or model boat-making room, if that speaks to your hobbies more directly?

What if you had a dedicated scrap-booking area? I imagine it tidy, gleaming, and ready for you to drop into in a minute when a spare half hour opens up.

Wouldn't that refresh, relax, and satisfy your creative urges better than half an hour flopped in front of the TV, or roaming aimlessly around the house being pulled at by dozens of misplaced or useless items?

Be not afraid to look at your rooms with new eyes. They are there to serve you, not live up to some outdated floor plan.

I overheard two women at a meeting saying, "We just need to get organized to get those books written and published..." and a light bulb went off in my head!

I thought, "That's it!! You don't just get organized to be organized; you get organized to do things!!"

Do hobbies, do passions, do projects; do R-and-R. Organization is there to serve you, not rule you.

Picture this: It's a free Saturday and your house is organized to within an inch of its life. No loose ends to feel guilty about. What are you doing today to enjoy and live this Saturday to the fullest? How could you do that every other day as well?

Read on

Why declutter?

When you've got that in place you are organized for the best of your life!

The first tip is the most important: declutter the guilts first. Your guilts arise from any number of compelling influences. Depression-era frugality, or post-World War II consumerism (seen as the answer to our war-torn economy), or keeping up with the Jones', or just the exuberant human tendency to take up more pursuits than we can comfortably handle.

Guess what? Nobody cares. Have some fun analyzing, but don't beat yourself up about it. By the time you figure it out, you could have had the hall closet AND the garage sorted!

The second most important tip is this: Never underestimate the value of decluttering and organizing. The time you spend getting rid of clutter, and organizing what's left so you can put your hands on whatever you need in less than a minute, will pay you back hundred-fold.

That 5-6 hours a week is basically the 55 minutes a day it's been estimated that we Americans lose, looking for stuff we can't find. Even if you did nothing more "useful" than stare into space* for those 55 minutes a day, I guarantee your life will be better, calmer, more focused, and more productive!

Research shows the top way to relieve stress is to clean out a closet! Given the buzz of energy and light-heartedness, I feel after cleaning out a closet, even when it's one of my clients' I'm sure it's true. It's a gift that keeps on giving, 'cause every time you look back at the closet you get that thrill again.

Stagnant stuff drags us down to an almost unbelievable degree, which only becomes evident when it's cleared out.

Imagine if your workspace or entire home were all as streamlined as that closet!

* Staring into space is a form of meditating, which is very productive...

If you have a guideline to follow when doing something, it'll make that activity so much easy. Same applies to Decluttering. This whole exercise will be done according to the following guidelines; they are basically the rules of the game.

Let's look at them

Guideline 1 – Visualize

Paint a clear picture of the end results in your mind. This will set a clear goal that you aim to achieve at the end of this activity.

Guideline 2 – Money

Target to make some money at the end. Money is the best motivational factor. It is an exceptional tool that could bring you to places, or help you and your family with household expenses and everyday living. You could even add up to your savings and emergency expenses.

Guideline 3 – Take action

Thoughts will make you think about it happening but action will make it happen. Simply the definition of power is "the ability to act".

Guideline 4 – Organize

The items that you declutter have to be organized into five piles. There is a need for a strategic and systematic method for decluttering that would lessen your usage of time and allow you to be more specific and detailed with your plan to divide and compartmentalize the essentials from the garbage.

Equipment Needed for Decluttering:

- You will be needing garbage bags, boxes, writing markers, dust rags, and scissors.

● Start by labeling the boxes (as instructed in Chapter 6: 5 Piles)

● Prepare a timer and set it for the corresponding time required (Chapter 5: Guideline 3; Take Action)

Declutter as quickly as you can and do not pull out more items than you could actually clear out for the specified period of time. Meaning, go through only one area, room, a closet, one drawer, or one furniture at a time. Don't do it all at once! Decluttering is supposed to be fun and an inspiring process that you would love to do all over again.

Now with the garbage bags and boxes fully prepared before decluttering, you could start by using a dust rag, wipe/clean, and get rid of things that you decide don't belong in the area you have begun with. Label the boxes designated as storage for the stuff to be decluttered.

Once the timer stops, you must discipline yourself to stack away the garbage bags and boxes to make room for other priorities and schedule in your life. But of course, don't forget to empty all those bags to be used for your next session of DECLUTTERING until the whole process has been completed. Check how fast you could do all these!

Guideline 5 – Digitalize

Prepare a location for incoming papers that usually become a part of the clutter. The reason for this is that we place them in several spots all over the house, on the table, chair, bed, top of the drawers and closets, or even inside the car. It's all scattered and messed up. Sometimes our papers pile mountain high because we don't have a good storage for all these.

We could create simple folders with labels separating the major bills and other paper works, place them in one area specified only for this alone. Such system may not have to be perfect but also store a few extra filing folders and labels just in case you have to create a new file. I am referring to hard copies of your papers and documents. However, there's another excellent way to put your papers and house in order.

Aside from designating a file box, another perfect strategy is to digitalize. If you got mail, school papers, receipts, manuals, notices, important flyers, you could have it all scanned and saved through a digital storage method. This minute change could work wonders and transform your paperwork.

This will help you keep a considerable amount of items without disposing because it's a clutter-free storage method.

Guideline 1 - Visualize

Do this at the start of the process.

As I said earlier you should have the result in mind, then you know where you're heading. Furthermore, it's the most enjoyable way to start the process because you're free to imagine what the end result will look like.

When I am decluttering my home or workspace, I take a few minutes looking at the room and thinking about how I want it to look later on. I ask queries such as, "What are the most important pieces of furniture? What does not belong in this area? What must be placed here or there? Do I love this item? Have I used it in the preceding years? Is it considered trash? I probably have another similar item that is better? Should I keep two same items at once? Does this item have any sentimental value? Or does it bring me feelings of guilt and sadness every time I see this particular stuff?

Visualizing how the room will look like if not cluttered helping me rethink and plan which must be considered non-essentials and have it all removed in no time. Visualizing actually worked wonders for me and I hope it will do the same for you. Another wise tip is for you to clear out your home with everything that makes you feel angry, guilty or sad and keep only what makes you happy. If you don't love something and only becomes a sore in the eye, then throw it! It might be loved by someone else.

For example, think of a container and before you open it visualize what should be in it. Then once you open it remove what you didn't imagine. It's that simple.

Some things you'll remember because you get a negative feeling by seeing them. I also suggest you remove them from the container. Once this is done you have a clear picture in your mind what should be in the container.

Apply the above to any area we do Decluttering for.

But there is something you must always keep in mind

> *"Do not dispose any item before checking whether it's needed!!"*

The last thing you want to do is to regret that you threw away something just because you overlooked it.

You could also start a no-clutter zone, which could be a counter, a portion of your couch, kitchen table or work table. Clear this area and wherever you may start, make a fixed rule that nothing could be placed in that spot that is not important. Everything in this area must be cleared and put away. You could expand on this slowly each day until your no clutter-area has spread through the whole house and you discover that you were able to declutter the whole house in no time.

Here's another fun fact, if there are days that you don't feel like working on a major decluttering session during weekdays then you could schedule it on weekends and even get your family and friends involved. The more helping hands, the better. Not only are you decluttering but it will also serve as a bonding time with those closest to you while educating them how to live an organized and clutter-free lifestyle.

Tip! – You can even draw a rough picture how your decluttered rooms should look like. This will motivate you further to take a strong effort to declutter because you have a clear picture of what you're aiming for.

Guideline 2 - Money

As I said earlier this is the best motivational factor.

Think of this as an incentive you'll get by Decluttering all the unused stuff.

Pause for a bit and do this. Visualize all the stuff you haven't been using but can be made use of by someone else in the middle of your drawing room. For each item picture the cash notes which matches its second-hand value. Do this for all items. In the end, you'll have a bundle of cash in the middle of your drawing room.

You might think you have paid more for these items than the amount you are getting and I totally agree. But remember this clearly "something is always better than nothing."

The money you make by selling this stuff can be used to fund something useful for you.

Where do I sell this stuff??

Well, you can simply start with your friends and family they might have a need for the stuff you have no need for.

Or else a garage sale would do. If you prefer to sell online the following sites are the most popular ones to sell used items.

1. www.ebay.com

2. www.amazon.com

3. www.craigslist.org

4. www.gumtree.com

5. www.etsy.com

You can even use a combination of all these modes. There is no hard and fast rule, whatever works for you is fine. But make sure to use a mode where you can sell this stuff for the highest offer in the shortest time period.

In addition, social media sites such as Facebook, Twitter, Instagram, Pinterest are powerful tools to get an audience or clients who would be interested in buying your stuff and help you to be clutter free in no time!

Another brilliant idea is to create a blog site through Wordpress.com or Blogger.com by writing stories and narratives to make your advertisements more attractive through the use of pictures and graphic arts. Not only will you be earning extra cash and profit but you will also have fun in letting your creative juices flow through building these web tools which could be used on a temporary or permanent basis or most likely whenever you feel like selling more things in the future. All these could also be multi-functional if in case a friend of yours would love to declutter then you could also earn by letting them post their personal or household items via your sites and help them live an organized life.

While some of your stuff may be categorized as "pre-loved or second hand" and may still be worth selling, all of your other things that people wouldn't buy may still actually be sold at the junk shop. Hence, money is made out of your extra things since what is garbage to you, are actually treasure to others.

Guideline 3 - Take action

There is an old saying that "a plan without action is a dream wasted". This principle is true for everything in life. I have personally made this mistake myself for so many things in my life and Decluttering has been one of them.

The previous two guidelines which I showed you are guidelines to have the correct mindset to start, continue and finish off this exercise, but this guideline is what makes it different and unique, with the end goal of accomplishing the plan to DECLUTTER.

You may have tried Decluttering previously or this may be the first time you're trying to practice it, but whatever the situation maybe there is one simple thing to keep in mind. You need to allocate a specific time of the day to declutter and you must declutter during that time. If I explain a bit more what you need to do during that time is to get rid of ten items you don't need in the allocated area of your house.

You may have the doubt that you don't have ten items to get rid of in that place. For example, if you started with your bedroom go through all the items thoroughly one by one trying to find 10 items you need to get rid of. If you didn't find 10 items you need to get rid of after thoroughly going through then that's fine but remember if you just skimmed through and didn't find 10 items then the exercise is pointless, simply because the clutter from the items you have missed will still remain in your bedroom.

The other side of the coin is not spending 30 minutes. I understand you have a lot of commitments and are pressed for time. That is natural. All of us have that problem. But that can be compensated by spending two 15 min time slots or three 10 min slots within the day. You can even split this into two days with only 15 min per day. Either way, make sure you spend 30min on an area. You might think that's too much time to spend. But there is a huge reason behind this; the simplest reason is you'll have to go through the stuff toughly. Having the commitment to do this for only quite a few minutes every day and completing the same doesn't sound to be that heavy. Decluttering could be fun and productive once you've set your mind to doing this.

Imagine this for a bit, if you have a file cabinet with a huge set of files that contain old documents you don't need you can just assume they're virtually useless and you can just throw them away but in an instance whereby some hard luck it contained an important document you disposed of, then there is no way that we can get it back. That's the hard truth we have to face. This is a cleanup exercise that we have to do with great care.

Been said that this is an average time period decided after doing this exercise for many times. If you don't have that much stuff and have thoroughly gone through one area then you're completely free to move on to the other. Going through toughly is the main rule of the Decluttering game.

The clue here is to take it one step at a time, you could have your own pace in performing all these depending on your available schedule. Then don't break the momentum. Continue the habit of decluttering for a few minutes every day. This book is all about helping you produce results with the inspiration to make decluttering look more like a hobby rather than a job to perform.

Guideline 4 - **Organize**

This'll make the process extremely easy and extremely neat.

Make five piles as follows:

1. Trash

2. Sell

3. Donate

4. Unsure

5. Keep

It's a simple and basic task to use two 15 min time slots or three 10 min slots within the day or that other option to split this into two days with only 15 min per day, locating items that would go to either of the five piles. For a day, you could look for 10 items to throw away, 10 items to donate or 10 items to sell. This is a really fun and easy way to immediately organize at least 30 items in your house. Or make this as a challenge to other members of the family so that they could also participate in your process of decluttering.

1. Trash

These are literally all the useless items you have in your home or office.

Some examples of these are old receipts, scrap paper, old toys, worn out clothes, rusty furniture or household items, unusable crafts, old wrapping etc.

All these must go to the dustbin without any mercy.

When doing this you'll find some stuff which you keep as Souvenirs, for example, a wrapper of a chocolate you had with a close friend. If so put all of them together and transfer to the keep pile. But remember this – if you are doing this for about 100 wrappers or other Souvenirs like this, you really need to rethink. Otherwise, the whole process will be in vain.

For the meantime, as we begin with our project of decluttering, while you are collecting and prior to dumping, one of our simple techniques is you could either grab or use a plastic, large trash bag or box to organize everything that you consider as trash and place this in one spot of the house where it could be easily seen and within your arms' length together with all the other four piles before throwing away or selling. While much of what you'll be collecting are trash, these containers could also be used as a bag for goodwill or even giveaways later.

2. Sell

These are items that are no more useful to you but will be useful to another person and can be sold for some reasonable secondhand value.

As an example, we could take children's books or teen books which you no longer read but another person in that age or who has siblings in that age will be interested in. Other items that could be sold in yard sales are clothes, planners/ journal notebooks with still enough space to write on, toys, household goods, furniture that you could repaint later on, arts and crafts materials that you have held on for so long and haven't used, chairs, tables and gadgets such as cell phones, television or DVD player.

You will never run out of cool stuff to sell that other people would find attractive. Some people store collectible items and vintage arts and crafts goodies. If you have any of this, this will sell huge amounts of money in the market or even over the net. Your clutter is someone else's treasure!

3. Donate

These are items you want to give away for free or in other words to charity. But remember these must be stuff which someone can make use of. If you don't it's like dumping your trash in someone else's yard. If the items don't pass the donate test by being in a useful condition move them to the trash pile.

You don't necessarily have to sell and donate either is your choice. If money is more essential, sell is the action to take and vice versa. But a point to take note of is that's always better for someone to make use of these items if they are worthier than just going to the trash pile.

You could try Colleen Madsen's idea at 365 Less Things where she gives away one item each day. This is a fabulous and brilliant method of decluttering and over the past years, she has reduced her stuff and even made other people happy by donating cool things rather than throwing at the trash and even made new friends along the way. Nothing beats a cheerful giver!

When your "Donate" box becomes filled up, immediately seal and close it and put it in your car so that the next time you get out of the house, you could donate the same to your local thrift stores. Always keep in mind that you are getting rid of clutter and not relocating it in another part of the house. This will definitely defeat our purpose for decluttering! Get rid of it! So after you have filled a box, go get another one and continue decluttering.

4. Unsure

This pile will be a large pile when you do this for the first time you'll have a lot of items which you won't be sure of keeping or giving away or throwing away. But don't be alarmed about this. Keep those items in this pile for a temporary period of no more than three months. While keeping this pile gauge them and move them to the relevant piles accordingly. After three months' time trash them once and for all. Be sure to keep these in a box, you don't want them to get mixed up with the other items.

Put a label on the box and write down on your notebook about the contents of the box so that it would be easy for you to review and go back too. You won't also forget that a box such as this still exist and, so you could get rid of the additional clutter inside it.

5. Keep

These are the only items you'll be left with. All items in the above piles are going to leave your house.

So, gather all these items carefully and cautiously, because you don't want to give away or trash what you really need.

Another extremely important point to remember is that sometimes an issue arises when after decluttering for hours or days, all the items just come back because we continue to buy more stuff from the market. So, while you are decluttering, do your best to fight the urge of buying and accumulating items which are not necessary in the first place. Take a minute to create a 15 days or 90 days list in case every time you would want to buy something new and not needed, you put it on that list. Create a rule that you will never ever buy anything that's not of primary importance. The list may serve a two-fold purpose, one that's essential and one that's not. Not only will you save yourself from additional clutter but also save yourself with extra cash and money.

Here is a list of items that you could keep and how:

5.1 Decide on the clothes you would love to wear: As you prepare for your job or day's work, visit your closet as you look for something to wear and spend a few minutes removing the clothes that you haven't worn for months. Do this religiously and consistently with your drawers and closets until only the stuff you wear is what's inside your clothes rack.

5.2 Clear out your medicine cabinets: Check out your first aid boxes or cabinets for pills and bandages, go through what's outdated or expired and stuff that you know you'll never use again such as old and worn out bandages, creams, and ointments that you are allergic too and keep only what's essential.

5.3 Declutter and Unclog your drawers and cabinets: Take the drawer and pour out its contents on the table. Then segregate the contents into 3 divisions:

    a. stuff that must remain in the drawer

    b. stuff that must be kept elsewhere

    c. stuff to put in the trash or for donation.

Clean and wipe the drawer, put back the essentials in order and then deal with whatever you have removed.

All these are only a few of the things that come into play. The sky is the limit in this decluttering project. You could think out of the box and be as creative and innovative as possible. I am here to give you ideas, to teach you how to start and the rest is up to you to declutter.

Guideline 5 - Digitalize

Some items don't need to be in physical form for you to make use of them. Letters, photos, and documents can be scanned. You can even take pictures of them.

CD's, DVD's can even be converted to digital form. You can use cloud storage to store them in a safe manner where they won't ever get lost and you can access them whenever you need.

1. https://drive.google.com

2. https://onedrive.live.com are great free cloud storage options.

Go through all the items in the keep pile and the unsure pile to see what you can digitalize. You'll find out that there'll be a fair number of items you can save from the trash pile and keep without taking up space.

This can even be done for a library of books. It's just a matter of scanning, converting and organizing them into an eLibrary which you can easily access on your PC or Kindle.

But if you're using them as reference books and prefer to use them in their hard copy format then you need to rethink this a bit.

The main thing to keep in mind in digitalizing these items is whether their purpose can be secured when they are in that format. If you cannot make any use of them by digitalizing, then it'll just be a time-wasting exercise to convert them into a digital format.

It's all about keeping them in a clutter-free convenient form to get the best use out of them.

Be reminded that you must always have back up or extra copies of your file. Another smart idea is to keep these soft copies through an external drive with a huge memory. Even your collection of movies may be kept in USB form so instead of having a scattered pile of DVD's or CD's, you have it all organized in an internal storage ready to watch in just one click.

Do not be overconfident of the fact that once you have fixed your space, it's already done. No, you're not. Be reminded that though you have started a new, efficient and logical method for managing and organizing outgoing and even incoming stuff and items, that is not the end. There is no such thing as an autopilot, hence you have to be consistent with the regular clean-up and upkeep of your home. The great thing, however, is that you now have an upgraded and updated strategy to process all your clutter. Once you get the hang of organizing and decluttering, it becomes a hobby, a part of your system that produces positive results in your life.

Let's get started!!

The guidelines I showed earlier illustrated how the entire Decluttering process works and how you should go about it.

Now we are getting down to business by taking action.

Only a limited number of individuals have home organization with drawers and closets which look like those in the TV advertisements. What the media feeds us are not always true. Truth comes out that reality speaks otherwise. I have been in various homes and I have seen how other people have reorganized their spaces and it does not look like what we see in commercial ads or TV home shopping channels. Though all these look awesome and dazzling, these spaces are used by human beings and not one that has been designed by marketers and a team of organizers for non-existent residents. It may be pretty, but the question is, how functional are these arrangements? You will only end up disappointed if perfection is your ultimate focus.

Our primary goal is to set up a home that works smoothly with all your needs, one that is real, applicable and systematically functional. With that in mind, we could proceed with our DECLUTTERING project and have a

100% assurance that we will be very successful in our endeavors to acquiring a life free from mess and clutter!

What are the areas of your house that must be decluttered? Here's a short list to check every now and then:

- Decluttering your Bathroom

- Decluttering your Bedrooms

- Decluttering your Closets

- Decluttering your Computers, Offices, and Workspaces

- Decluttering your Entry Way

- Decluttering your Kitchen

- Decluttering your Living Room

- Decluttering your Papers and Mails

General Game Plan – Tips 1-19

1. Where are you now? Take a clipboard or legal pad, or whatever, and walk around your domain, noting which areas get on your nerves with clutter or lack of organization. Take 'before' photos.

2. Now, figure out where you want to go. Is it:

> **a.** A home that's just shy of model home beauty, showing off your artwork and style instead of stacks of stuff?

> **b.** Army barracks minimalism, with nothing holding you back from an action-packed life of adventure???

> **c.** A cozy family abode with room for cozy family activities?

> **d.** The restful haven to recharge from your hectic life?

> **e.** Just some noticeable improvement over the current chaos?

3. Find the vision that inspires you. For instance--imagine yourself as a tycoon. Your home office has a desk as big as Kansas, only the current piece of paper you're working on visible. The rest is tucked neatly away, or being handled by your "people!"

4. My favorite general vision is the well-stocked vacation condo; nicely decorated, basic necessities there, no clutter. It gives me a refreshing springboard for my vacation adventures, or distraction-free spot to work on the Great American Novel.

5. Can't think of anything? Write down ten things you'd like to do in your ideal workday and leisure day. What would your home look like to support those days?

6. Review favorite organizing motivators. Just because it didn't work totally, that is, you still have some clutter, doesn't mean it, or you are a failure. (See 'Declutter the Guilts' again.)

7. What works best for you, the carrot?

    a. Carrot: It's Saturday, the house is in perfect order, and you and the troops are footloose and fancy-free to do whatever you like.

    b. Carrot: Organize the living room, and create a perfect spot to spread out the $1000 worth of chrome you just bought for your motorcycle (True story.)

    c. Carrot: It would be so yummy if your house operated smooth as cream...

8. Or stick:

  a. Stick: You find mold growing in someone's bedroom.

  b. Stick: The item you just broke your ankle on has been sitting on the stairs, waiting to be put away, for approximately six months.

  c. Carrot and Stick: your turn for the book club in three weeks. Theoretically, they truly love you for your brilliant literary discussion. But still, you want the house to look storybook perfect.

10. Tackle the worst first. Back at your clipboard, identify the area of the house that bugs you the most. You'll start with that one; it will have the quickest positive impact on your daily life. Mom always said, "Make up the bed—the biggest item in the bedroom—and you'll be ready to attack the day!"

11. Still not sure? Consider:

  a. The "basement," or other long-term storage space. Then there's room to put things you've pared down to.

  b. Entrances, to avoid stressing out visitors or family as long as possible.

c. Kitchen, or home office—wherever you spend the most time.

d. Point is, just start somewhere!

12. Schedule the time to declutter and organize. Think you just can't stop to do that 'cause you're just WAY too busy doing life? Well, let's face it. You have all that mess 'o stuff now because you didn't take the time before. If someone offered you $500/hour to organize, I'll bet you'd find time to squeeze in! Keep remembering those 5-6 hours a week. Eventually, you'll break even...

13. With the snag that bugs you most, whittle away at it between your scheduled times, if a window of time opens up. Put away a few items. Ask yourself what's one small thing you could do daily to shift it. The relief from handling the worst area will make the rest of your list look easy to deal with.

14. Get some help, Part One. Turns out the part of the brain that comes up with good intentions: "I'm getting rid of 90% of my junk" (!) is not the same part that makes a plan to get it done. Pair up with a friend and sort both your arenas together, or just call each other to make sure you're staying on track. Reminders keep us remembering our intention.

15. Get some help, Part Two. Hire a professional organizer. Wouldn't dream of inflicting your mess on your friends? A professional organizer may know some shortcuts that would make the process ever so much quicker and more painless. The cost is reasonable, and the motivation of having an appointment with someone, and paying them money has a galvanizing effect on the process. It gets done!

16. Sell expensive items you don't cherish anymore, through free classifieds and consignment shops. This is where an organizer can help, too. They often have resources for getting your stuff sold.

17. You could have a garage sale, but don't do it on my account, unless you have an ocean of stuff to sell, and garage sale season is either in full swing or just a month or two away. Those things sitting in your house waiting for months is not what we're looking for here!

18. Fear not; remember this reassuring truth: All organizing projects basically boil down to three steps:

Sort, purge, organize what's left,

OR,

Purge, sort, and organize.

If you're good at making quick decisions, purge first. If not, sort first, to see how many of each item you really have. This makes it a little easier to let go of your thirteenth through twenty-second white shirts.

19. Also, the clutter really is finite, regardless of how big the mountain seems. It just looks impossible because you're stuck in the first place, with all that stagnant energy.

Feng Shui Basics - Tips 20-22

20. Every feng shui treatise known to humankind recommends uncluttering your spaces. Feng shui philosophy (It's not a religion, just FYI.) states we are always interacting with the objects around us. This is pretty much what quantum physics says, too, so how about that? Even if you don't get any farther than "uncluttered" in your feng shui attempts, you'll have handled the biggest issue.

21. This explains why we most always feel dragged down when we enter a cluttered space. Those objects that have become forgotten, thus essentially useless, are latching on to you in an attempt to gain some of your energy for themselves. Did I really say that? No, I couldn't have, but there is something weird about how we lose our zest when we are around stagnant stuff. Observe your reaction next time in a messy place, and also how much more energized you feel in a calm, uncluttered area.

22. The modern American feng shui motto is, "Love it or use it; otherwise lose it." Anything that is not cherished, or regularly put to use is automatically clutter and needs to leave.

Decluttering Basics – Tips 23-26

23. Move everything out of the space you are decluttering; whether a whole room, or just a single drawer or closet, remove all the items. Even if you end up putting many of the items back, as they really are used or loved, you will still have released up that stuck energy. By considering each object you put your mind at ease about the things you're keeping.

24. If you can, put kept items back in a slightly different place. Just this small step will refresh the space as well.

25. Make one of your goals to clear off all flat surfaces. Kitchen counters were meant for preparing tasty meals, not storing every scrap of paper that enters your home. Dining tables are for congenial meals, not ten years worth of tax records and catalogs.

26. The floor is the ultimate flat surface, and Feng shui is pretty firm about keeping the floor clear of stagnant storage, to maximize your flowing energy. Think: dancing, kids, and pets running around, a temporary space to lay out your cat-fishing gear for today's expedition.

Good reasons to get rid of stuff - Tips 27-42

27. Old, outdated, un-cool clothing which has somehow shrunk in the last five years—Even if you do lose some of that weight, you'll be wanting something refreshingly up-to-date to go with your refreshed new attitude!

28. You're so kind, you'd love to pass those unwanted items to someone who will use them regularly. They get the stuff and you get the stirred-up, frisky energy. Win-win!

29. And! All the fossil-fuel energy that went into producing that stuff is now redeemed, not moldering on your shelf.

30. You spent a fortune on that stupid gadget, so why not send it along to someone else? Thus you shed the reminders of your less-than-excellent decisions.

31. You could make some money.

32. You will also shed negative emotions about the past and fear of the future. Late Aunt Mabel will not mind that you give away her knickknack. She's having fun, and knows you won't forget her! Nor will you be so destitute in the future that you won't be able to replace that one item in a hundred you are storing "just in case."

33. It's the fastest way to streamline your life and open it up to amazing new possibilities.

34. Decluttering is the hardest part of organizing for most people, as we must then make the decisions we've already been putting off. Don't make it harder by beating yourself up about your indecisiveness. Just keep telling yourself, "I've been busy!"

35. How to decide what send to its next home? If one of the above reasons doesn't resonate with you, just keep asking yourself whether each item supports or takes away from the vision you came up with earlier.

36. Or, (Stick, big time): Your house is threatened by a natural disaster, and you have an hour to take out what you value most. What would go with you and what would be left behind?

37. Then there's (Carrot, big time): Imagine you won the lottery, and for some strange reason had to stay in the same house. Would you keep everything you had now, knowing you could easily afford whatever random item you might need in the future?

38. Take a leaf out my friend's book. After a 6-week trip to Belize, she came back in shock. "I thought I knew how to do without (from the way I grew up), but these people really know how to do without!" Don't underestimate your ability to improvise with what you've already got. It's better than you think!

39. If you're the logical type, realize you can't put 15 inches of books into a 12-inch wide shelf. Group the books in fives and pick out your least favorite 1 or 2 from that group to get rid of. With less pain, you can weed out your lower-status-treasures, and methodically reduce the load.

40. If you like competition, see how many garbage bags you can fill up to toss or donate, in a couple hours' time, or as compared to your decluttering companion. (You both win!)

41. Always leave time at the end of the decluttering session to send stuff to its next spot—misplaced items to their correct rooms, trash bags to the curb, donations in the car to be dropped off at your earliest, etc. Otherwise, your feeling of accomplishment will fizzle out once you lift your head from your decluttering frenzy!

42. Too late? Already drooping? Take a ten-minute iced tea break, move away from the area, re-focus on that "pared-down condo" vision or whatever floats your boat, then go back in and tackle the distribution.

"Clear the space and feel the rush!"

Organizing Basics – Tips 43-51

43. Organizing principle – go vertical wherever you can. This will reduce not only clutter in your field of vision, but also take up less floor, desk, or shelf space.

44. Humans are naturally drawn to either order or display in what's pleasing to look at. They can combine, such as a uniform set of dishes stored in a clear cabinet, or a bulletin board jam-packed with info tidbits, artwork, and cartoons. In general, err on the side of austerity as you complete your organizing. You'll probably be adding some things eventually…!

45. When life is in its extra-hectic stages, simplifying possessions, such as keeping matching glasses in the kitchen rather than a hodgepodge of different styles, will help reduce stress.

46. A lot of organizing seems to consist of sorting belongings that have become jumbled or out of place. Just the simple act of grouping like items, and putting them away in a logical place, will give a quick sense of peace and order.

47. Use your head in deciding where to store instruction manuals. You're unlikely to frequently need to look up how to use your refrigerator, eh? So keep that manual in your filing system. However, if the DVD player won't co-operate, frustration will be loud and instant--create a little pocket very near it for the manual.

48. Ditto when it comes to deciding whether to have multiples of items or just one. You'll be surprised how much a pair of scissors and a roll of adhesive tape stored in three or four places around the house will come in handy. Cleaning supplies in every bathroom reduces resistance to that dread chore. You'll likely only need one baby grand piano, though. See how easy that is?

49. Be realistic about the storage space you have. Good for you if you've managed to pare down a quarter of your wardrobe! —However, if your closet only has room for 60 percent of your current inventory, it's still going to look stuffed! Your choices are: create more storage (Work...yuck!), or, pare down some more (better.)

50. Whenever possible organize with a view to providing dedicated areas to explore your hobbies. Ready access to a good set-up increases chances of following these life-enriching interests, rather than flopping down in front of the boob tube, cause it's too much hassle to round up the right equipment and find a spot.

51. Cut out pictures from a magazine of space decorated and organized the way you like it. Post it prominently for yourself. There are few things more effective in helping you stay focused than seeing your dream in front of your face often.

The Parking Garage – Tips 52-57

52. What organizing book starts with the garage?? Bet that shocked you! Well, this one does, because for many of us, it's the family entrance to the house. What better place to start decluttering and de-stressing than the first place you see every time you come home? It's not out of line to think of painting the floor or finishing the walls. Of course, that would require getting a bunch of stuff out there first, wouldn't it?? Hmm....

53. Need another motivator? In most homes, the vehicles are the most expensive possessions. Are they being stored inside or outside?

54. To really reduce visual garage clutter to the minimum, store all the long-handled tools, both gardening and cleaning, as well as the skis, etc., standing upright in a clean trash barrel, like the toothbrush cup in the bathroom.

55. If there's a workshop area in the garage provide it with good lighting and heat, so it's inviting to use.

56. Be realistic about what your family really plays with or uses. If the handyman supplies all perfectly arranged on the pegboard never get touched, but there's an active gardener in the family, toss the handyman stuff in a labeled box or bin, and hang up the gardener's hats instead.

57. Camping, skiing, or other gear-heavy pastime your family's thing? Dedicate a big shelf with no competition adjacent to the vehicle that gets used to take you there.

The Mailroom – Tips 58-67

58. Stock the mailroom with three trash cans, one for trash, one for recycle, and one to shred. Make sure the recycle one has plenty of room!

59. Keep three nice containers handy for when you bring in the mail. Magazine files work well (look like cereal boxes with a slant cut through the top and down one side), or you can use squarish baskets, in-boxes, or substantial bags that will stand up by themselves. Make sure whatever it is, is spacious and sturdy.

60. The mailroom could be a small secretary table by the front door, a station in the laundry room if it's next to the garage, the desk or cupboard in the kitchen, or even in your home office! The key is: make it handy enough to go to the second you come in the house with the mail. No setting it down on the counter— "for now"!

61. The first container is for the days you feel organized enough to sort the mail immediately. Recycle everything you can first. Next put time-sensitive materials, like bills and incoming checks--Hey, it could happen! --in the first container, and whatever materials you do want to read/save into the second. Take shred stuff directly to the shredder.

62. The third container is for the days you just can't face doing any of it, so dump it all in there. At least you've kept it tidy and contained, rather than spreading all over the counter. Resolve to clear it out every 3-4 days, so it doesn't grow to an overwhelming volume.

63. The next stage for the mail is deciding what to do with it. A small file box on the desk with room for just a few hanging files bridges the gap between "piles" and "out-of-sight, out-of-mind." They could have labels such as:

a. "High Priority"

b. "Pending," - for plane tickets, and 'waiting for info from someone else'

c. "To File"

d. "To Pay"

e. "To Read"

f. Other custom files for your own business or family

g. "I don't know" – Get back to these when you're in a more decisive frame of mind.

64. Think twice about "To File"—Can you get the info again from the internet easily; will you really ever look at it again? Could it be scanned?

65. "To File" – Part 2. A fabulous, super-easy to use filing system is the key to not ending up with a depressing pile of "to-be-field's"—If possible, whatever has passed the test of # 64 should go immediately into the file!

66. The key to handling the desktop file categories is to enter the actions into your to-do system, whether online or on paper. They can be grouped by categories, such as "Computer," "Calls," "Errands." Putting stars by the time-sensitive and very important tasks helps the get done in a timely fashion.

67. To reduce the influx of mail:

a. Eliminate magazine subscriptions – read online, or at the library

b. When you order an item online, see if you can check a box to avoid getting sent "offers and catalogs"

c. Go to: dmachoice.org (direct marketing association) and click on "Direct Mail 101" to get your name off lots of mailing lists.

Go to: optoutprescreen.com to eliminate credit card offers for either five years or life.

(Both of those sites should show "https" in the browser for security.)

Home Office Strategies – Tips 68-73

68. First, and foremost, make sure the office and its furnishing/décor match your personality, not somebody else's idea of how offices should look. You may, or may want to, spend a lot of time there, so customizing it for your work style will make the time much more enjoyable and efficient.

69. Pare down office décor to just a few things, Feng Shui-inspired or otherwise, and definitely something that makes you laugh! It may seem austere, but you'll be way more productive, relaxed, and less distracted. Think, "Tycoon!"

70. Get everything you use on a daily basis in your office within arms' reach. Move seldom-used manuals or other info into a different room, so you can focus on your hot projects with no dead weight around.

71. Make your filing system as simple as possible but still functional, plus, reflect your style. You may feel more comfortable breaking out all your user manuals by brand name, for example, or prefer to throw them all in one file. Your call.

72. Similarly, consider color-coding your files. It's a very powerful tool, if you keep things simple enough to maintain—you know, yellow for family, blue for "Taking Care of Business" (insurance, etc.), red for bills, or whatever.

73. After trying all the filing methods ever, I ended up with one file drawer for "fun stuff"—"Restaurants to Try," "Kid's Writing," etc., and another for TCB (taking care of business). They are each alphabetized, but the colors are a rainbow on steroids. I found it bugged me to have the "Health Insurance" folder mixing in with the "House, Dream" file, so now they're separate.

The Kitchen – Tips 74-80

74. Of all the rooms it's important to keep organized as well as clean, the kitchen is right at the top. Food served from a messy, dirty kitchen is unappetizing, plus keeping it clean discourages pests of the non-human variety.

75. No matter how OCD it may seem, keeping spices in alphabetical order really saves a boatload of time, not to mention finding belatedly you have five jars of curry powder, when one at a time is, really, all you need.

76. If you like to have help in the kitchen, set it up with an eye to convenience, even to the point of having extra knives and cutting board in a second location for a recruit to chop up veg for you.

77. If you'd rather do it all yourself, then set it up with an inscrutable logic only you can discern and invite guests to relax in a nearby armchair (I have one in my kitchen, even though I do like assistance. Well, actually I prefer to sit in the armchair, and let someone else cook…)

78. Go through every gadget, fancy pan, and custom appliance you have and ask yourself if its function could easily be duplicated using some simpler item already on the "A" list in your kitchen. Try packing it away in a less prominent, but not impossible, location for six to twelve months. If you haven't really missed it, then....

79. I tend to favor simplifying the view in the kitchen as much as possible. So, I would personally steer clear of the glass-fronted dish cabinet concept (Unless it has glass shelves and translucent backlighting!) But you must please yourself on that point.

80. Most people naturally group items for baking, food storage, drink or snack items in their own 'departments.' Ever thought of bagging up all the little packets you get with take-out food--mayo, ketchup, salt-and-pepper, plastic flatware—and adding them to the picnic department? Who knows? They might actually get used up!

The Bedroom – Tips 81-87

81. You've heard it before, but it's worth repeating. The bedroom is for rest and relaxation, a retreat from your hectic life. Resist the temptation to fill it with mini-home offices, televisions, libraries, wet bars, etc. The bedroom is the best place in the house to keep it simple.

82. Alas, feng shui will tell you that keeping things stored under the bed interferes with your restful sleep, and love life. If you must use that handy area for storage, try to keep it very low-key and soothing, like extra blankets and bedding.

83. In Europe, it's common to clothe a bed in a bottom sheet, pillows, and a duvet—nothing else. It's incredible how easy it is to make up the bed in the morning, and the duvet cover can be washed periodically.

84. Color-coding your clothes makes it easy to see how many of each color garment you have, thus perchance, also making it easier to let go of some of the over-represented tones.

    a. Some people color-code by grouping all the items of one color together--easier to put coordinated outfits together in a hurry.

b. Others group them in broad, general categories, like long-sleeve shirts, short-sleeve shirts, slacks, jackets, etc., then line up each category in rainbow order.

85. A big time-saver, especially if you don't tend to get your clothes very dirty in the course of your day, is to have a substantial inventory of socks and undies. Believe it or not, it is sometimes humanly possible to air out your outer garments and hang them back up! You wouldn't believe how long you can put off washday by doing this. (So good for the environment.)

86. If there's room, have a hamper for colors and one for whites, or some other division that makes sense for you.

87. Ever heard this packing-for-a-trip tip? Pack one outfit for each activity anticipated, then put half of it back, and you'll usually end up with just the right amount. What if you applied that same philosophy to your wardrobe?

The Lounge –a.k.a., the Bathroom – Tips 88-92

88. Consider letting each person in the family have their own color of bath towels, washcloths, etc. Also, each member over the age of eight gets to learn how to do their own laundry. Not only does this teach a valuable life skill, it saves dozens of hours a year sorting.

89. I'm not a big fan of a mis-mash of bottles of products stashed anywhere and everywhere in the lounge. Try limiting yourself to only those with non-toxic ingredients. This will cut your choices down to an astonishingly small number, and do your health a huge favor. Did you know your skin absorbs more toxins from your environment than the rest of your body put together?

90. As with everywhere else in the house, an excess of stuff strewn around in the bathroom slows people down when they enter, thus encouraging a lot of dawdling in a room, that, while tremendously important, is not where you want to hang out for hours...

91. A couple baskets on the counter can corral a lot of small, miscellaneous items, plus be decorative. A little bouquet of silk flowers or a candle or a painting helps convey the spa/vacation condo ambiance, reminding us we have fun adventures to get back to.

92. Isn't there something about a clean bathroom sink that makes up for a lot of other lounge clutter sins? Keep a sponge or washcloth handy to wipe down the sink and faucet every day. Takes 30 seconds and pays big dividends amid the chaos.

Maintenance – Tips 93-99

93. The ingrained tendency to clutter up flat surfaces in a fierce one, so be prepared to act with resolve to resist.

94. Do what you can to make order-restoration fun, or at least highly-motivated. Leaving the TV off Saturday mornings till the kids' rooms are tidied up will ensure it gets done in record time; either that or they'll miss an entire morning of cartoons, which isn't really that bad.

95. Give yourself your own competition to see if you can put away 75 items in, say, fifteen minutes.

96. You may just have to be kind, but firm with friends who attempt to give you their unwanted items to soothe their own guilt about the stuff. "I just don't have the room!" should be your ever-ready response. This is how the uncluttered pros do it.

97. Remember to take photos of your space once you get it all decluttered and organized and compare them to the ones you took when you started. Pat yourself on the back for an amazing, and often difficult accomplishment! Also, post them to remind you of your ideal, and inspire you to restore, if necessary...

98. It's inevitable, in the bustle of daily life, that things will start to pile up again. Make a pact with yourself to relentlessly keep at least a couple of areas, such as the kitchen and master closet, tidy. Then, at least every 3-4 days take half an hour to an hour to restore order in the other parts of the house, so it doesn't get away from you again.

99. Most of all, live in the present instead of the past (Too many mementos keep you anchored there.) or the future ("I might need it someday.) The energy you free up by living for today will help make you more successful in every area of your life and inspire you to live the best of your life!

Game Plan Part II – Tip 100

100. Take 3 of those alleged six hours a week we spend looking for lost items and use them to gradually get your house ship-shape. Then take the other 3 hours for a fun outing or session with your favorite hobby. Thus, you model for yourself whittling away at a project, AND, using the time freed up to follow your passions.

Thanks for reading. Have a super time getting yourself sorted and organized for the best of your life!

Day 1

First, take a notebook to note down the items you have. This'll make the whole exercise extremely easy. Choose a place to start. You can choose any area of your house. Just make sure you start with an area which you'll be comfortable with. Don't start with a difficult area because you will get stuck during the process and will want to give up or procrastinate, I'm not trying to demotivate you but its natural I have been there myself!

I recommend that you create a list of places or spots in your home to declutter by starting with the easiest. Now when you're done with one area, then STOP. You have the choice to make your list as easy or difficult as you wish for it to be done depending upon the places in your home that you are including in your list (e.g. rooms/ closets/ drawers/ cabinets). Your specific schedule to work out on this plan may also be included in this list.

Let's say for example you started with your bedroom, now to make things easy and organized we will start with one corner of your bedroom. Let's go from one end to the other. Let's say you started from the left top corner of your bedroom. Go from the left top corner to the right top corner, then from right to left. You'll tackle the room in a zigzag manner.

You need to make sure that you are opening every cupboard, every drawer, and every container. Now before you open a cupboard picture what you need to have inside as I mentioned in the visualizing guideline. Let's say for example you start with a cloth cupboard in your bedroom. Now before you open it imagine what should be in there. Let's say for example the following items should be there,

Tip! - If you find imaging it difficult at first to form the most expensive item to the least expensive item, you can do vice versa. Anything that works for you is fine.

I'll be going from the most expensive item to the least expensive item and

*Remember the following list is just an example. Your list could go on for any number of items you desire; there is no barrier for it.

1. Formal suit - 1

2. Jackets - 2

3. Trousers (office) - 3

4. Shirts (office) - 3

5. Trousers (casual) - 4 / Jeans - 4

6. Shirts (casual) - 4 / T-shirts (casual) - 4

7. Belt - 1

8. Tie - 1

9. Socks – 4 pairs

10. Shoes – 2 pairs

Now take the notebook I mentioned earlier and divide the page into two. On the left side put the heading as "assumed" and write all these items down. You might wonder why I am doing this like an inventory count of a company. Well its simple, it'll leave all the burden of the Decluttering exercise on the notebook and not on your brain. So you won't have to take too much stress on it.

Now you can see that we have imagined and written down 10 items.

Open the cupboard. And put the heading on the right side as "actual" Go through all the clothing items and write them down. You don't need to write down each and every item of the items which are in pairs. For example, if you have three pairs of socks you don't need to write as pair 1, pair 2, and pair 3. If you just write 3 pairs of socks that's more than enough, and it will save a lot of time.

You just need to find out what you have exactly. After going through all items in the cloth cupboard you'll have the list you "assumed" on the left side and the "actual" on the right side. Now if both lists on the left and right sides are equal the cupboard doesn't need to be decluttered, simple as that. But sadly, the probability of that happening is very low. Most of the time you'll find a considerable difference.

Remember the 5 piles:

1. Trash - T

2. Sell - S

3. Donate - D

4. Unsure - U

5. Keep - K

For short I have given a letter in front of each pile, let's use them.

You don't need to have both sell and donate piles you can have the one you prefer as I mentioned earlier.

You can start by considering all the items in the assume pile as the ones which fall into the keep category. But if you're having any second thoughts go through the assume list, but I'll start with the actual list to illustrate how this is done.

Go through the list in 5 stages and get the help of the "assume" list to decide on which items you need to keep.

Stage 1 - Go through with the objective of finding and marking "T" for the items you want to "Trash".

Stage 2 - Go through with the objective of finding and marking "S" for the items you want to "Sell".

Stage 3 - Go through with the objective of finding and marking "D" for the items you want to "Donate".

Stage 4 - Go through with the objective of finding and marking "U" for the items you are "Unsure" of what to do.

Stage 5 - Go through with the objective of finding and marking "K" for the items you want to "Keep".

Remember all the things I explained earlier, don't have any bias when you do this if you do then this entire exercise will become pointless.

Once you're done you don't need the assume list. You know what to do with each item.

All the items with K in front of them should stay inside the cloth cupboard.

Apart from that pile up all the items which have T, S, D and U separately. You can even put them into boxes if it's easy for you. Make sure they won't get mixed up again.

Continue doing so for the other areas in your bedroom from left to right for the remainder of the 30min.

Now you're left with the T, S, D and U piles. What you must do immediately is to trash all the items in the T pile.

The S (Sell) and D (Donate) piles leave your room. Find a location in your house to keep them for a temporary time period. Treat them as guests who will leave in a few weeks' time and the room they stay in is their guest room. Keep the unsure pile in the corner of your room.

Make use of your imagination to help in decluttering objects you find difficult to remove. Ask unique queries such as "If I would buy this, how much do I have to pay for it?". These are additional techniques that will provide assistance when it comes to obliterating clutter.

We are pretty much done for the day. And if you want to take a whole day and complete this exercise in one go, no problem but make sure you take a break after doing this even for an hour because you're thinking all the time during this exercise and it will mentally tire you and during the latter part you'll find it difficult to concentrate on what you're doing.

Day 2

Let's repeat the same steps till trashing the T pile and moving the S and D piles to their location.

Then take the previous day's unsure pile and review it and see whether you find any items which should be trashed, sold, donated or kept. If so, move them to the relevant pile they should be in.

Setting our goal on minimalism requires the above techniques in order to declutter certain areas at home. I have personally tried these methods and it all worked out for me, my family and friends and I am hoping that it will be the same for you. As I have planned to declutter, I used five boxes: trash, sell, donate, unsure, and keep. No item was left behind, each one was considered diligently and carefully. Some projects took hours, some days and others, weeks. However, the style and principle remained similar.

Here's the point of the matter, no matter what style or method of technique you choose to help you get started with, the first and foremost goal is to take gentle and first steps with initiative and excitement. I promise you that there is a breath of fresh air behind every clutter and the freedom to enjoy greater space and more profit. It is your choice and decision how you clear it all up.

Day 3

Now you have done this exercise for 2 days and you can see a change happening in the areas of your house you have done this.

This can be rounded up to three things:

1. The clutter in your room is starting to disappear.

2. You are having an increasing pile of items you can sell or donate.

3. The unsure pile in the relevant area is increasing (but, if you are transferring items to the T, S, and D piles then it'll decrease or remain static).

If the above-mentioned changes are happening you're on the correct track and you must proceed with consistency and delight.

There are levels in decluttering. It may be that your home is already neat and all tidied up but there will always be that certain area that has been cluttered with non-essentials such as old paper mess that must be thrown out or your medicine cabinet that you haven't cleared out of expired pills and ointments for more than a year and has to be sorted out.

This guide will accommodate you in whatever level of decluttering you are in. This Guide is applicable to any kind of clutter and mess you have in your home whether there be only a little amount of mess or it's the disaster cyclone type of clutter.

Day 4

Continue the same exercise as usual and let's assume you have finished the Decluttering process for your room by this day and have revisited the unsure pile as well.

Now what you need to do is focus on the S (Sell) and D (Donate) piles. You need to tap your friends and relatives, post these items on garage sale websites such as

1. www.ebay.com

2. www.amazon.com

3. www.craigslist.org

4. www.gumtree.com

5. www.etsy.com

For the items you need to donate, you can tap some of your friends or relatives who might be able to make use of them or you can give them to your church or any nearby charity organization which will direct them to people who can make use of them.

You might be able to find people or places to sell donate these items on the same day but generally, it'll take a few days or even a month to sell or donate these items. But they will not be cluttering your room anymore.

Keep in mind that you must complete each task 100%. After sorting things out by category, the crucial part is letting go. Never have second thoughts of keeping boxes for charity and friends to deliver "later". The key to decluttering is "Do it now!" Complete the process, take the plastics or boxes to trash or recycle as soon as possible. Now, if you're planning to donate or give away items, put all of it immediately in your truck or schedule up for dropping them all off. You've already separated the items, packed them up for disposal, so better complete the whole deal.

*Remember sometimes you cannot get the price you expected for the items you're making an effort to sell. Then you're left with three options:

    1. Sell them at the rate you receive.

    2. If no one wants to buy them donate them.

    3. If you can't find a person or place to even donate them, which is very rare send them to the trash pile.

Never consider the option of keeping them, "that will definitely clutter up your room, and take you back to square 1!!" These items must somehow leave your house within one to two months' time. Please don't misunderstand my being assertive but my responsibility is to give you a strong guideline and make this exercise productive.

Please don't procrastinate doing this, because this will generate some money for you. Some have the preconception that the target of Decluttering is to free up space and trash all the items you don't need but, that's a wrong concept and an incorrect way of looking at it.

As I told you in the introduction "this is a practical exercise that will benefit you by removing clutter and generating some money" the two objectives must be achieved for this to be a success.

If you solely donate and don't wish to sell, then I encourage you to set your objectives as removing the clutter from your house and helping others.

Either way, this exercise will serve a meaning full purpose.

As we have stated earlier, other modes of selling your clutter are through advertising on social media sites where thousands of people go to, to invest, buy or sell brand new and pre-loved goods. For the stuff you think would still benefit others then take a picture of the same. You don't have to be a professional photographer in order to achieve this, a simple picture with clear lights and bright background will do. After doing this, post the pictures of your items at any of these sites:

1. Facebook

2. Pinterest

3. Twitter

4. Instagram

5. Personal Blogsites

Having done this, add up a caption with a clear description of the goods you are selling. If there are imperfections or slight damage, also add it up to the description to show the buyers that you are in good faith and you have integrity with your words and they will surely buy from you the second or even third time around. Don't forget to put the price. If you are open to haggling, then state that the item is "negotiable", so the buyer or client may find that you are easy to communicate with and this will give you leverage as you sell your items. Your buyers will see you as approachable and easy to deal with and they will keep coming back to you for more items to buy and keep.

Repeating the same steps

Now you can see that we have cleared one area of your house in four days and we have done the following without bias to all items in that area:

1. Clearly classified what items are useful to us and what we are going to keep and we kept them.

2. Clearly classified what items we can sell and make money, what items we can donate and help others (both of these or one of these) and sold and donated them.

3. Clearly classified what are the items we need some time to decide what to do with and reviewed them in an ongoing manner till we disposed of them in three months' time.

You can now move to the next area of the house. There are only two things you need to do for the area of your house which we finished.

1. You need to go through the unsure pile in your completed area once a week and move any items which need moving to another pile accordingly.

2. You need to follow-up on the advertisements you put for the Sell items and sell them and deliver the Donate items to the people who you wish to donate them to.

Now moving on let's assume you have

3 Bedrooms

2 Bathrooms

1 Living Room

1 Dining Room

1 Kitchen

1 Garage

So if we assume it takes 4 days to declutter each then...

3 Bedrooms - 4 days x 3 = 12 days

2 Bathrooms - 4 days x 2 = 8 days

1 Living Room - 4 days x 1 = 4 days

1 Dining Room - 4 days x 1 = 4 days

1 Kitchen - 4 days x 1 = 4 days

1 Garage - 4 days x 1 = 4 days

Total = 36 days to Declutter your home and another 54 days to remove the Unsure pile.

So literally you'll have a clutter-free home in three months' time. Simple as that.

But remember all of the above are average guides. For example, if you live in an apartment you can do this in less than half the time.

And if you want to trash the Unsure piles in the house on the same day you finish Decluttering the last room that totally up to you. I won't give a strict guideline for this because it's totally up to you, to do what's comfortable for you. But keep in mind not to compromise the practicality and productivity of this exercise.

Take note that you also shouldn't be too hard on yourself. Do not spend the whole, rather, the entire day organizing your whole house. Only a few individuals have the time, energy and focus to spend 8 to 10 hours fixing, decluttering and organizing. You might become frustrated and less efficient if you work for ten hours straight, decluttering. You will not feel tired, wasted or even burnt out if you follow our guidelines on the number of minutes or hours to spend in accomplishing your decluttering project. By doing this, you will feel more encouraged, inspired and motivated to work your way through.

This is the goal of this book, to help you enjoy decluttering your home and to lessen the load of having to achieve freedom through a balanced perspective coupled with productive style and techniques in decluttering. I am here to help and once you have seen the success of your endeavors, you could also share this article with someone else in need.

Watch Out For These!!

So far I have illustrated the practical method to declutter your home. I have written other books on organization and simplifying your life which I have been passionate for quite some time and I have come to think that most of my readers share my same thoughts in having an uncluttered house or office workspace, but they just don't know where to start.

I am sharing not only my heart with this book but also my experience. When your home is filled with so much clutter and a pile of mess, it becomes an overwhelming task to remove and re-organize.

So how do we start? Here's my simple advice: *Start with 5 minutes.* Small and baby steps would do you a greater good later on. That five minutes wouldn't finish half of your clutter but it sure is a great way to begin! Once you have started, it's time to celebrate since you have broken the status quo of living a life in clutter. This is the beginning of a new and excellent chapter in your life. Mess-free, clutter free!

The next day will be a whole lot easier, take another 5 minutes tomorrow, then the next day and before you know it, you have cleared your bedroom, kitchen, dining area or even half of your house! It's like a game you play, only this time, you will reap amazing and productive results.

There are some things to watch out for as you go along. These are all very important matters to discuss so please focus 100% on the following:

1. Bias ness

Never be bias when deciding on an item to leave your home either through the trash pile, the sell pile or the donate pile. It will only add to the clutter. Think objectively rather than thinking emotionally.

Now don't misunderstand this as I am instructing you to throw away photos that have the sweetest memories in your life. All the lists I have given are pure examples. What is important to you is not the same as what is be important to another person. The only thing to keep in mind is that you need to make your best productive unbiased judgment. Memories and keepsakes, we believe couldn't be replaced and accompanies certain events or wonderful stories of your life and your family's. You could find a way to keep all these either through digitalizing or by putting up boxes assigned particularly for memoirs. Just don't overdo it. Always take note that we are working on DECLUTTERING and you have to cross out the unnecessary items, stuff that clogs up your home and makes it look like a mess.

2. Keep consistency

This exercise in general terms will take 30 minutes of your time for the first month and then till we dispose of the unsure pile will take about 10 to 15 minutes of your time. I know you have commitments and some days you won't be able to allocate your time for this. That's inevitable; you must allocate time for these commitments. That's totally understandable but don't use that as an excuse to procrastinate on this.

3. Always use the help of the notebook

At first, as I earlier mentioned you might not feel the need for this but remember as I earlier stated this would put the entire burden on the book. At the end of the process for each room, you will know what you have and what you have decided to do with them or rather did with them during the process. You might even be surprised at what you have in your house.

Another side to this is that you'll know where you unnecessarily spend on useless items and need to cut down. This will make a considerable impact on your spending habits and help you to save money that can be spent on more important things.

The notebook serves as a record of what you have accomplished for the past days, decluttering your home, going through one room and closet at a time. Since sometimes, our memories fail us, the notebook will come up handy in times of need. This will help you track down your improvements and stick to the plan of decluttering. For a more fun outlook on this, why not add a touch of creativity as well in creating a notebook most especially for this project alone. Add up color and a bit of art and crafts so that writing will not feel like a school assignment but a hobby that you look forward too.

In the end

So, we have come to the end of this guide to Decluttering. I hope you are clear on what you need to do, how to do it and what to watch out for.

This is a short guide and the reason why I didn't write a lengthy book on this aspect is because I wanted this to be an action plan for you which will impact your life in a positive way by making your home clutter-free. My personal theory for this or any change needed to be made in life is that the plan or rather

"The action plan is 2% and the action is 98% of the change you need to make"

This is the philosophy I follow in my life and this has helped me immensely and it will do for you as well.

Another idea to keep in mind is that sometimes the problem is not only because of us but it's the individuals we live with inside our homes. A home that is not cluttered is organized and free from the mess is a clear showing of shared ideas by all the people living in the same residence. Speak to your housemates and let them know that you desire to live in an uncluttered home. Do this with much grace and persuasion instead of sounding like nagging or scolding. Explain how fun and enjoyable decluttering could be for the whole family and the results it will effectively produce in one's life.

Another thought

This might be something you're already thinking

"Can't Decluttering be used for my life as well?"

Well, certainly it can. And it'll benefit you in a much more than Decluttering your home because your home is just a part of your life.

You are in control of making that decision to declutter as often as you like and need. You could do it every day and you could even make use of a timer. However, this habit might become a driving force that leads you to be compulsive. It might happen that once you begin, you would want to clean out everything all at the same time. Don't! You might burn yourself overworking and going beyond what you could accomplish. Everything has limits so only perform decluttering one small amount at a time. Do not forget that your house did not get messy and dirty in just one instance, so you cannot clean it all in just one night. Setting a timer would help you time yourself and not go overboard. Totally decluttering your house may not be attained in a superhuman speed, but it is achievable through carefully laid strategies and methods just like a puzzle that you form into a bigger picture later on.

The clutter in your life is the cause of:

1. Stress

2. Anxiety

3. Moodiness

4. Depression and

5. Anger

Been free from them can make you live up to your full potential. This, I will be covering in another book.

Finally, ...

Thank you very much for taking time to read this book. Hope it will transform your home into a clutter-free home which will be cozier. If that is done, then my objective of writing this book is achieved. Once you get the hang of decluttering your house, you could move on clearing up your computer and even your workspace. Having learned a systematic way to organize the messy and chaotic home, you now have the knowledge of creating a technique in decluttering all the other areas of your life.

Thanks again!!

"It's not the daily increase but daily decrease. Hack away at the unessential." - Bruce Lee

Conclusion

Like what I have stated earlier, decluttering doesn't have to be perfect, it has to be simple, enjoyable, fun and functional. You don't have to be a genius to achieve and accomplish beautifying your own home and organizing the same with style and grace. You will even be astounded by the benefits you will be rewarded as a result of your organized and clutter-free life. The profit you could earn in decluttering will also be the fruits of your labor and even extend into helping others in their financial distress.

You could hear testimonies of people who have had breakthroughs in life when they took one small step towards letting go of the clutter that they hold on too for years. One of those amazing stories could be yours. Picture yourself in a clean, organized and clutter-free home. Even your family and friends will see that change and would want to even live in your house. People will start asking how you did this or that and they'd look to you for advice and guidelines. Who knows, you might even write your own book or article one day and become the guru of decluttering.

You hold your future, you hold your life. Decluttering your home is one small step to a successful life. It holds true that an organized home is an organized mind. Having the knowledge to organize and compartmentalize stuff and items is a gift that only a few people have, and it could be yours from this book. Don't you find it pretty going to places with all the tables, doors, chairs, utensils in their proper places? Don't you want to live in a place where everything is in order? Once you have set your house in this manner, look at the greater possibilities you could achieve in your school, office and even the community. Have you ever thought that being a person with greatness, starts in as simply fixing your bed?

I remember a high-ranking military official once said to his clumsy and messy subordinate "How could you change the world if you couldn't fix your own bed?". This is genuinely true. You cannot help fixing other people's mess and bring about a change in their lives if you couldn't fix your own little mess.

Just like your home, it is also empirical that you take an extra mile to declutter your own computer or business (if you are engaged in any commercial venture) in the exact same method that we started to declutter your home. In addition, I am very much pleased to announce that I have started working on writing a few more dedicated books regarding these topics in order to help you further.

Now that you have read this book, it's time to put every principle into action. As you become successful in this project, don't forget to share this book with others and let them know that decluttering is an easy and doable task. So, put your chin up because you are only minutes away from getting the freedom that you desperately aspire for, the freedom from a messy, disorganized and clutter filled life. Enjoy this journey with me as we take it step by step to a clutter-free home!

Thank you and good luck!

Chloe S

Printed in Great Britain
by Amazon

41260060R00149